Monograph 45
The American Ethnological Society
June Helm, Editor

URBANIZATION
OF AN AFRICAN
COMMUNITY

Voluntary Associations in Bamako

By CLAUDE MEILLASSOUX

UNIVERSITY OF WASHINGTON PRESS

Seattle and London

Preface

SINCE 1960, and following their struggle for independence, the government and people of Mali have undertaken a difficult and courageous task of political and economic construction. In this new context, the voluntary associations, which were the result of the abandonment in which the city people were left during the colonial period, have lost a great deal of their importance, now that the government is trying to fulfill the needs of the townsmen in a more orderly and educative way. Indeed, as we shall see, all the voluntary associations are not appropriate means of integration into the city milieu, and the official concern over providing for satisfactory alternative institutions is legitimate. However, the attempt to make the official associations compulsory and exclusive has not yet been completely successful; voluntary associations have shown up again, but they exist today in opposition to the over-all party system, compared to which they are of limited scope.

The main point we want to stress, is that Bamako society, as it is perceived through the voluntary associations described below, is not fully accounted for, and that our study ignores the valuable and strenuous efforts of thousands of young men and women, organized in the "Jeunesses de l'U.S.–R.D.A.," to build a progressive society.

This work is dedicated to those young men and women, as a measure of the ground that must still be covered and as an encouragement for what they have already achieved.

Acknowledgments

THIS study has been made possible because of the interest of the government of Mali in scientific research. I am grateful for the help and understanding of President Modibo Keita, who, in spite of his numerous duties, kindly agreed to discuss my work during my year's stay in Bamako; M. Madeira Keita, Minister of Justice and a talented social anthropologist; M. Singaré, Minister of Education; Seydou Tall, Director of Cabinet; and M. Idrissa Diara, Secrétaire Général of the Union Soudanaise. Thanks are also due to the officials of the Ministry of Foreign Affairs; MM. Kase and Traoré; to the Director of the Institut des Sciences Humaines, M. Amadou H. Ba, and to his staff, particularly M. Youssouf Cissé; to the Director of Statistics, M. Yaya Diakite, who gave us complete facilities; to the Director of the Interior, M. Cissé; to the Director of the Museum, M. Moussa Sy; to the former Director of the Lycée Askia Mohamed, M. Bakary Kamian; to the Mayor of Bamako, M. Soungalo Coulibaly; to the Secrétaire d'Etat à la Fonction Publique, M. Oumar Baba Diara; and to the many others who gave me much of their time and sympathy.

I also want to thank my friends from Niaréla, especially my host, M. Abdoulaye Touré, and his family, who suffered my

vii

blunderous intrusion for a year and gave me in return the warmth of their unforgettable hospitality. I am grateful to all the officials of the associations described in this work for their friendly help and welcome. Special thanks are extended to the late Amadou Coumba Niaré, to whom I owe most of my knowledge of his people and society; to the *sous-section* of the Union Soudanaise in Niaréla and to its officials, MM. Bomboli Niaré and Ibrahima Kante, who smoothed things over for me many times, and to Gaoussou Camara, who was my efficient associate and friend during my pleasant and happy stay in Bamako. Many thanks are extended to Professor Paul Bohannan who directed me with this study and who eventually struggled through my approximate English to straighten it out for publication, and to Susan Messerley for keeping my morale up through her cheerful and helpful mail.

CLAUDE MEILLASSOUX

Paris

Contents

Illustrations and Tables

Part 1

BACKGROUND
OF CITY ASSOCIATIONS

CHAPTER ONE

Bamako:
The City and the People

THE HISTORY OF BAMAKO

ACCORDING to a partial census taken in 1960 (*Etudes démographiques* 1960), the city of Bamako numbers about 130,000 inhabitants. Small in relation to Western standards, it is still by far the largest city in the Republic of Mali. While the urban population (people living in towns of 2,500 or more) accounts for only 6.8 per cent of the total population of Mali (300,000 people out of 4,370,000 in 1962), Bamako makes up 44 per cent of the urban population (Amin 1963:1).

Population of Other Malian Cities
(over 15,000 inhabitants)

Kayes	35,000	Ségou	29,000
Kati	32,000	Koutiala	25,500
Timbuctu	30,000	Sikasso	21,500
Koulikoro	29,000	Mopti	18,000

See map 1; Source: *Etudes Démographiques* 1960.

When first visited by the French in 1888, Bamako was a village of eight hundred or one thousand inhabitants. It was the leading town of a small chieftainship comprising about thirty villages on the left bank of the Niger River, with a total of about five thousand people (Vallière 1888a). The leading

3

clan was the Niaré, which had come eleven generations before (between 1640 and 1700) from Diara, Kingui, an ancient kingdom located in the North, itself created by the Niakaté—ancestors of the Niaré—after the dispersal of the Sonīke from the old empire of Wagadu (Meillassoux 1963).

Soon after its foundation, Bamako attracted *Suraka* (Moslem Moors) from Touat, marabouts and merchants who settled under the protection of Niaré warriors. Little by little the place came to fulfill several of the functions of a city. For defense against their neighbors, and especially against the armed slave raiders, fortifications were built—a *tata* (banco wall) ten feet high and seven feet wide, flanked by twenty angle towers. A permanent army of *sofa* (cavalrymen) was raised with which the Bamako people overcame the rival clan of the Diara, formerly established in the area, and put several neighboring villages under their domination. They formed alliances with other chieftainships, mostly with the clans Coulibali and Diara (different from the one mentioned above), which reigned in succession in Ségou. Though they took part with that kingdom in a few military campaigns—against the Diakité from Samaniana or against the Manīka people—Bamako was assaulted only once and enjoyed comparative security.

During the dry season, caravans from Mauritania came and settled under the walls of the town to exchange their merchandise (salt, cloth, arms, horses, and cattle) for slaves, and to a lesser extent for gold and native crafts. The Niger River was an obstacle for the Moors, who could not cross it with their camels. Beyond the Niger, Sonīke and Jula traders took over the traffic, on foot or with donkeys, and carried trade farther south, toward the forest. Bamako, like a few other towns on the river, took advantage of this site to become a fairly important marketing place (Park 1954:181–82). A slave market was held daily inside the walls, as well as a weekly fair. This trade made the wealth of the two local Moorish clans, the Touati and Dravé, whose influence was becoming greater.

Because of the growing importance of traffic on the river and of the need for fishermen, the Niaré settled a group of *ba-moxo*

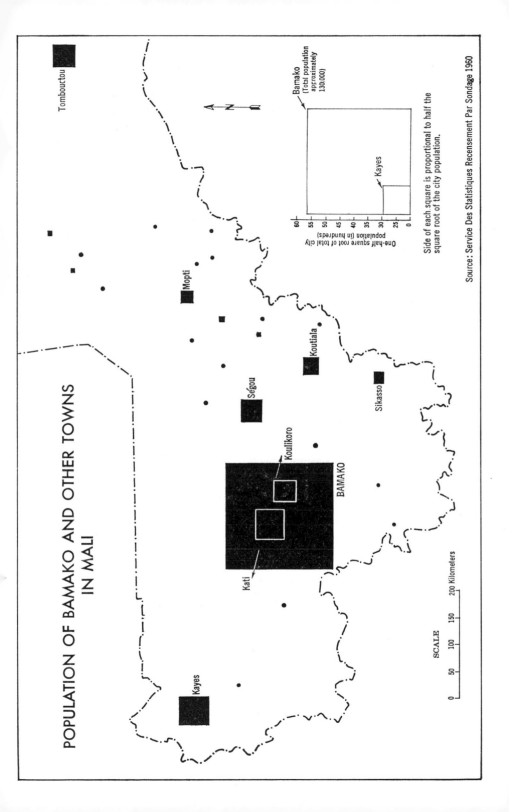

POPULATION OF BAMAKO AND OTHER TOWNS IN MALI

Tombouctou

Mopti

Koutiala

Ségou

Sikasso

Koulikoro

BAMAKO

Kati

Kayes

Bamako
(Total population approximately 130,000)

Kayes

One-half square root of total city population (in hundreds)

Side of each square is proportional to half the square root of the city population.

Source: Service Des Statistiques Recensement Par Sondage 1960

SCALE

0   50   100   150   200 Kilometers

(river people), the Bozo and the Somono,[1] a few miles from the town. The leading Bozo family, the Djiré, had been taken in from a neighboring town during a raid against the Diara of Niamana. To increase their number, the three leading clans of Bamako entrusted the Djiré with captives, to teach them their trade. The descendants of these captives are said to be Somono.

Hence, the town was made up of four sections: Niaréla, Touatila, and Dravéla sheltered the three main clans, each of which was protected behind its own *jifutu* (wall); and later on Bozola was added when the Bozo took refuge inside the walls following an attack by Samory's armies (Meillassoux 1963).

When the French, who were settled in Saint Louis du Sénégal, decided to push in toward the Niger River and the Eldorado they believed was behind it, they chose Bamako as the main outpost to be created on the river (Ministère de la Marine 1884:7, 117, 187).[2] In 1881, Colonel Galliéni reached Bamako on his way to Ségou, where he expected to deal with Amadou, the Toucouleur sovereign. But Amadou was the enemy of the Bamana, and the latter attacked Galliéni near Dio, sixty miles from Bamako (Galliéni 1885:222). Fortunately for Galliéni, his guide, recruited in Saint Louis, was a member of the Dravé clan, and he found protection in Bamako. At this time the French were more warmly welcomed by the Moors than by the Niaré (*ibid.* 243ff.).

Two years later, Borgnis-Desborde came with a battalion to occupy the place. In the meantime Samory, then at war with

---

[1] The exact differences between the Bozo and the Somono are not clear and vary according to authors and places. In Bamako the Bozo are said to be an ethnic group with their own language and patronyms, traditionally engaged in fishing and boating activities. Whoever is engaged in trade and fishing and is not a Bozo is called Somono. The Somono, on the other hand, have no language of their own, and their patronyms belong to the neighboring ethnic groups— Bamana, Manīka, Sonīke, and so on.

[2] Actually, the river is navigable only farther downstream, at Koulikoro. But according to a report by Galliéni, a member of the French colonial army, the French feared that if they had settled as far as Ségou, which was the next convenient point and even more suitable as a capital, the British from Sierra Leone could have taken over the upstream portion of the river. Thus, geographical factors are not as significant as strategic ones in explaining the settlement of Bamako.

the French, had threatened the town. The Moors by that time
wanted an alliance with Samory for religious and political
considerations. The Niaré, fearing this alliance, sided with the
French. Borgnis-Desborde accused the Moors of plotting with
Samory and shot two of their elders, releasing therewith a
suppressed feud between the two parties (Méniaud 1931:I,
162ff.). In February, 1883, Borgnis-Desborde started building
a fort at Bamako. Soon afterward, Samory's lieutenant, Fabou,
besieged the place, but he was driven away after three battles
in April, 1883 (Galliéni 1885:209 *passim*, 243 *passim;* Ministère de la Marine 1884:221 *passim*). Bamako fell to French
rule. The French officials decided to put the Niaré in the
position of *chef de canton,* which they maintained until 1956.

During the time of the wars against Samory and Amadou,
Bamako remained a military outpost—a place of refuge for the
peasants from the right bank escaping the Samory's soldiers.
There was little activity. The French had forbidden slave trading in 1892, and the caravans deserted the town for fear of
being intercepted by the *gardes.* Political life inside the town
was dominated by conflict among the leading clans, which
could not break into the open under French rule. The end of
the Bamako warlords came with the pulling down of the *tata*
between 1895 and 1898.

Not until the defeat of the two enemies of the French (1898)
did the town begin to develop. A railroad was being built from
Saint Louis to Bamako, and workers were recruited in large
numbers from the nineties to the time the railroad reached the
town in 1901. The first train entered the station in 1904. The
same year a steamship company started to operate on the river
from Koulikoro, the end of the railroad line, eastward to Gao.
This same year the colony of French Sudan was created, and
Bamako was designated as its future capital.[3]

When the fort was pulled down in 1903, new administrative
buildings were erected on the hill of Koulouba, overlooking the

[3] Until then, the Sudan territory belonged to a larger colony known as the
Haut-Sénégal-Niger, the capital of which was Kayes, on the Sénégal River
(Méniaud 1912:112).

town. Simultaneously, European trade moved in and settled downtown near the railroad station. In 1904 the number of commercial establishments jumped from nine to twenty. They bought rubber, gold, peanuts, ivory, and hides, while they sold cloth, salt, hardware, and a great quantity of spirits. A Chamber of Commerce was created in 1906. In 1908 the government was transferred from Kayes to Bamako. Besides becoming the main administrative center, the town grew as an important through-traffic point supplying upper Guinea, upper Ivory Coast, and the areas of Bougouni and Sikasso. African trade did not lag behind that of the French. The kola trade took an upturn through the use of railroad facilities. Bamako became a transit station between the supplying market of Ivory Coast and the consuming areas of Sénégal. This was to remain the main trading activity of African businessmen in Bamako, and we shall mention it often.

The town began to take on the appearance of a city. The first movie theater opened in 1910. Electricity and water were first supplied in 1911, when street labor also began; a narrow-gauge railroad was laid between the main railroad station and Bamako harbor; a hospital was built on one of the hills overlooking Bamako; more trading houses moved in, and a brick factory, which was to remain the sole industrial plant until Independence, was erected in 1912.

Although these improvements interested the French colonists more than they did the Africans, the native population of the town also grew. The construction yards had first employed Wolof, brought by the army from Sénégal to build the fort. In 1904 these Wolof obtained permission to settle in a section of their own that took the name of *Ouolofobougou* (*bugu*, settlement). Many of them died of fever or returned home, but the name has remained, with only a few Wolof to justify it.

Natives from the surrounding areas came seeking employment as porters, laborers, and servants, or under compulsion. They settled in two earthen-built villages on the north side of the railroad. One, of evil repute, was called *Kolikotobougou* (the hoodlums' place); the other, *Le Campement*, took the name of the neighboring military encampment. Inside town, a settlement called *Kayes-Liberté* was reserved for the freed slaves, but it did not last long, as most of the inhabitants "escaped" from the French protection, which reminded them too much of their former condition (Bouche 1949–50).

By 1907 Bamako had about six thousand residents, and in 1912, seven thousand—still less than the historical cities of Ségou or Sikasso, each of which boasted about eight thousand people at that time. After the First World War, when more trading houses moved in and sought space near the station, the administration decided to make room for them, and between 1917 and 1919 chased the entire population into new areas, parceled out on the periphery. The African town was torn down, with the exception of Bozola; European buildings, mostly stores, warehouses, and administrative buildings, were erected instead. The aboriginal history of Bamako had ended.

The three main families were moved into distinct settlements which kept their former names: Niaréla and Touréla on the east side (today Touréla is officially named Bagadadji; the Touati clan had changed its name to "Touré"), and Dravéla on the west side. A little later, in the 1920's, Ouolofobougou was parceled out, while people from Le Campement and Kolikotobougou were moved into lots to make, respectively, the new sections of Dar-Salam (from the Arabic "the house of salvation") and Médina-Coura on the north of the town. These were the first seven sections of the new city: Niaréla, Bagadadji, Dravéla, Dar-Salam, Médina-Coura, Ouolofobougou, and the old Bozola.

From 1910 to 1960, Bamako, though located farther inland, grew at a faster rate than Dakar (which already numbered twenty-five thousand inhabitants) and Conakry, but not as fast as Abidjan.[4] This progress can only be measured through uncertain censuses or estimates. There are no details about the

[4] The relative growth of the above cities during the same period was as follows: Dakar increased in population 15 times; Conakry, 12.5 times; Abidjan, 28 times; Bamako, 20 times (*Annuaires du Gouvernement Général* and *Annuaires Statistiques*).

composition of the population before 1948. As we have seen, the growth was slow from 1881 to 1910. The growth rate rose about twice as fast from 1910 to 1947 (38,659 inhabitants) and took a sharp turn upward from then to 1960 (130,000 inhabitants).

Many buildings, including some of the most important in the city (the governor's palace, the hospital, and the other administrative buildings), were built before 1917. But with the establishment of numerous trading firms, the administration was increasingly aware of urban problems. In 1923 avenues were designed, trees were planted along the streets, and a market was built in the middle of town under the administration of Terrasson de Fougères. The new European city was the site of extensive road labor; all European sections were supplied with electricity. A broadcasting station was established in 1929, and highways were opened toward Guinea and Ségou. In the early thirties, forced-labor recruitment was intensified in order to contribute to the projects of the Office du Niger, and the French administration turned its interest toward the needs of the natives. A leprosy hospital was established, and native crafts were encouraged through the foundation of an Ecole de l'Artisanat and the opening of a *suk* (group of craft shops). But the effort was cut short by the devaluation of the pound in 1933 and the consequent drop in peanut prices. Until 1945 conditions worsened for the Africans, and the development of the city was slowed down. During the period from 1920 to 1945, the population grew more rapidly than during the preceding period. In 1920 Bamako had about fifteen thousand inhabitants; it remained at that level until the mid-thirties. It started to grow again after 1936, reached thirty-seven thousand in 1942, but no more than thirty-eight thousand in 1948 (*Rapports politiques,* and Archives, Mairie de Bamako). At that date the Bamana population still represented 47.5 per cent of the total population, Jula [5] 13.5 per cent, Manīka 8.2 per

[5] The term *jula* used in the census is not defined. It probably covers several ethnic groups engaged in trade: Manīka, people from Sikasso, Sonīke, and others.

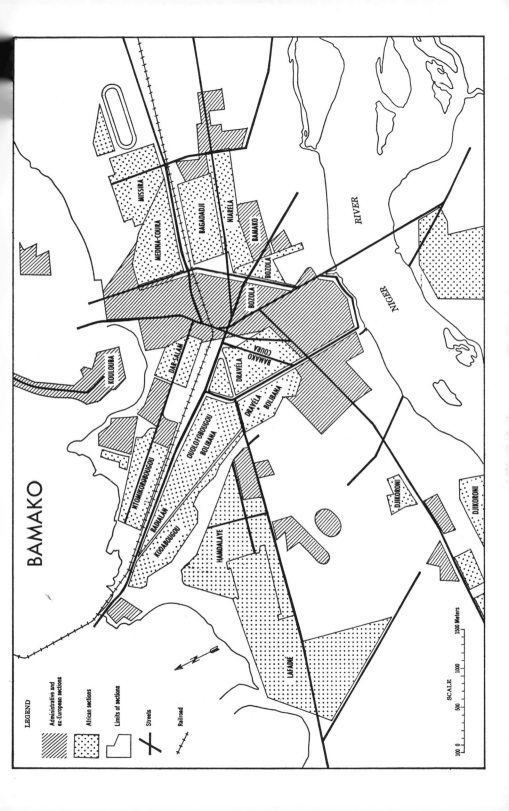

BAMAKO

LEGEND

- Administrative and ex-European sections
- African sections
- Limits of sections
- Streets
- Railroad

SCALE

100 0   500   1000   1500 Meters

MISSIRA

MEDINA-COURA

BAGADADJI

NIARÉLA

BAMAKO

BOZOLA

BOZOLA

KOULOUBA

DAR SALAM

BAMAKO COURA

DRAVÉLA

DRAVÉLA

BOLIBANA

N'TOMIKOROBOUGOU

OUOLOFOBOUGOU

BOLIBANA

BADIALAN

KODABOUGOU

HAMDALAYE

DJIKORONI

DJIKORONI

LAFADÉ

NIGER

RIVER

cent, Moors, 6.8 per cent, Fula 4.2 per cent, and Sonĭke 3.1 per cent. The Wolof constituted only 1.8 per cent and the Bozo-So-mono 2.5 per cent. The remainder of the population of the city was divided among more than fifteen other ethnic groups, among which one can mention the Miñäka-Senufo (1.8 per cent) and Voltaic peoples (3 per cent) (*Population Census* 1948).

The city also favored the extension of Islam: 88 per cent of the urban dwellers declared themselves Moslem, while the figure was probably lower than 20 per cent in the bush. To absorb the new settlers, the city at first spread slowly toward the east, which is both the way to Mecca and a propitious direction for the pagans. Soon, however, because of the swamps which lay in that direction, people started to move to the other side. The density at this time (1948) was 162 inhabitants to the hectare (approximately 2½ acres), and the most densely populated sections were Médina-Coura with more than 6,000 inhabitants, and Ouolofobougou, which now included Bolibana, with 5,437 people. Outside the city proper, small settlements were springing up, some of them to become future sections or suburbs, such as Kodabougou which had a population of 72 people; or Djikoroni, which is the name of a former village, with 193 people.

The European population more than doubled and grew to 2,853 people in 1947, as compared with 1,141 in 1940, while the African population scarcely increased during the same period.

The end of forced labor in 1946 and of the *régime de l'indigénat* (through which the Sudanese were "subjects" of France and not citizens), the launching of development projects that followed the war, the opening of the country to political life—all these factors contributed to start a period of prosperity and to initiate the real beginning of urbanization in the country. The rate of growth of towns over 2,500 inhabitants increased from 4.9 between 1929 and 1945 to 6.8 between 1945 and 1962 (Amin 1963:1). New buildings were erected in Bamako—several colleges, hospitals, and a hotel of high standard. Asphalt roads were built inside and outside the town; the bridge over the river was completed in 1957. Circulation of people and money increased, commerce developed, and native trade and crafts took a new upturn. Bamako became the main market for kola in Western Africa. Sudanese trading companies spread throughout West Africa. Bamako also profited indirectly from the growing export of dried fish and live cattle from Mopti toward Ghana and Ivory Coast, where coffee cropping had created a new demand.

The drive toward independence [6] spurred political life. Several elections were held, and Bamako became the center of the new parliamentary institutions. Party congresses and conferences were held there, and in 1955 the R.D.A.[7] Congress of all the former French territories met in Bamako. With the development of urban life and the growth of a social elite, Islam became the near-compulsory religion of all Bamako dwellers, and in 1957 an impressive mosque was built in the heart of the town.[8] The city began to be considered as a laboratory for urbanization. An embryo modern city was built at the approaches of the bridge. Parliamentary buildings were erected. At the same time, a poorer suburb, Badalabougou grew in disorderly manner on the other end of the same bridge, on the right bank, until it was partly demolished in 1962 to make room for better housing.

During this last period (1947–60) the population grew twice as fast as during the previous one (1920–47) and reached 130,000 inhabitants. Workers, government employees, merchants and peddlers, craftsmen, students, politicians and their families, and even invalids coming for cure contributed to this growth. People came from farther and farther afield, and the

[6] The first referendum took place in 1958. In 1960, the Federation du Mali, including Sudan and Sénégal, became independent. In 1961, the Federation broke up. The Sudan kept the name of Mali.

[7] Rassemblement Démocratique Africain, the party of the genuine African claim for independence, opposed to the Progressiste party (P.S.P.), which favored autonomy with the help of the French government.

[8] The French made some contribution to this building, though the greater part of the cost was covered by citizens' subscriptions. The attitude of the French colonizer toward Islam has always been ambivalent.

ethnic composition of the Bamako population changed. In 1960 the Bamana comprised only 25 per cent of the population, as compared with 47.5 per cent in 1948, but the Manĩka increased from 8.2 per cent to 18.4 per cent, the Fula from 4.2 per cent to 12.5 per cent, and the Sonĩke reached 10.6 per cent as against 3.1 per cent in 1947. The four groups total 67 per cent of the population. The other ethnic groups do not amount to comparable figures, as shown in Table 1.

TABLE 1

ETHNIC COMPOSITION OF BAMAKO POPULATION
(Computed from the data of the random sample census of 1960)

Bamana	25.5%	⎫	Dogõ	1.9%
Manĩka	18.4	⎬ 67%	Bobo	1.7
Fula	12.5		Sorko	1.5
Sonĩke	10.6	⎭	Moor	1.5
Jula	3.7		Somono	1.2
Kasõke	3.6		Senufo	1.2
Wolof	3.4		Mosi	1.1
Miñãka	2.5		Bozo	0.7
			Others	9.0
				100.0%

Though most people wished to settle on the east side, where rents rose, the bulk of the newcomers were directed toward the west. From 1944 to 1952 they moved into Ouolofobougou-Bolibana and Badialan, an area that developed along the southern side of the railroad. In the period from 1952 to 1955, they settled in N'Tomikorobougou, which is the former name of a village swallowed by the city. Hamdallaye (from the Arabic, *El hamdu-allah,* praise to god) attracted new residents from 1950 to the present, and after the bridge opened, they gravitated toward the right bank. The growth of the city has not stopped. The movement now seems to feed upon itself and is cumulative. The newcomers are content to settle farther and farther away—in Djikoroni or Badalabougou, and, since 1961, in the newest section of Lafadie (from the Arabic, "rejoice in God") beyond Hamdallaye.

Urban planners are now at work designing the city of tomorrow. They foresee a doubling of the population in the next twenty years, and an over-all density of two hundred inhabitants to the hectare. They intend to move all administrative buildings downtown between the present center and the river, toward the bridge entrance, and to build a university on the hill overlooking Badalabougou on the right bank.

Enough space is still available that Bamako will not become a crowded city for some time. Today Bamako spreads like a butterfly between the hill and the river, on both sides of the former European center, and along the railroad. On the two hills overlooking the town stand the administrative section, part of the former European residential areas, and the main hospital.

As is common in most African cities, housing in the European section drastically differs from that in the African sections. While the European housing consists of stories-high buildings or bungalows, the Africans live at street level in dwellings made of banco or of cheap building materials. In the oldest sections, the housing is the geometrical version of the traditional dwelling; the *du*. A square central yard, the *du-kene,* is surrounded by long, flat buildings the depth of a single room, each opening toward the center, under a terrace that runs all around. Though it may vary in shape and be more or less crooked, the general pattern is the same everywhere. In the newest section, however, there is a tendency to build houses in the European manner, that are a cross between the old style and the bungalow.

The *du-kene* is common to all the tenants. There women cook, wash, pound the food, and so forth. Farm animals—chickens, sheep, and even horses (though it is forbidden)—are kept in the *du-kene*. The dirt streets are large and wide, and play a complementary role in domestic life. There children play, women pound (sometimes in company) and, since there are no sewage disposal services, throw away used water. The streets are also the business location of the peddlers and the craftsmen; the weavers build their looms in the streets and work all day. At night people dance there or watch the *Koteba*[9] (see Meillassoux 1964) or other performances.

In spite of its rudimentary street construction, Bamako is clean and pleasant under the numerous trees that border its streets. Far from resembling a slum, the town looks rather like an overgrown village, designed according to a square, modern pattern.

THE POPULATION OF BAMAKO

In spite of its fast growth, Bamako is, demographically, a remarkably well-balanced city.[10] The sex ratio is slightly in favor of women (502 women to 498 men for the total population, and 501 women to 499 men for people over 15). If we consider only the age group over 15, we find more men than women only in Bozola (65 men to 54 women), Ouolofobougou (66 to 43) and Missira (148 to 136) where migrant bachelors settle more willingly. Everywhere else the sex ratio is even, or slightly in favor of women. The proportion of married people (over fifteen) is very high: 70 per cent for both sexes—80 per cent for the women, and 60 per cent for the men. The lone adult population (people with no family ties in town) accounts for only 15 per cent of the total adult population: men 10.5 per cent; women 4.5 per cent, among whom many are elderly women who are guardians of wards.

Socially, the people of Bamako are stable and family oriented. An appreciable proportion have been born in town: 25 per cent of the total population. In 12 per cent of the households the husband and one of the wives were born in Bamako. It is no surprise, then, to find a balanced age distribution, as shown in Table 2.

The age pyramid shows a bulge between fifteen and thirty for the women and between twenty and forty for the men, an effect of immigration. But the birth-rate trend, which is as high

[9] A farcical popular theater performed in the street upon private invitation by a troupe of amateurs.

[10] The following data have been computed by us from the random sample census undertaken by the statistical department in 1960, which covered one-twentieth of the Bamako population.

TABLE 2

AGE DISTRIBUTION OF INHABITANTS OF BAMAKO
(*Etudes Démographiques* [Bamako] 1960:4)

Age groups	Men	Women	Total
under 15	41.8%	39.4%	40.6%
15 to 59	53.2	57.1	55.2
60 and over	5.0	3.5	4.2
Total	100.0%	100.0%	100.0%

as it is in the bush, will make this bulge less conspicuous as time passes.

The above data provide evidence for the fact that the migration of men into town is soon followed by marriage, often to a country girl (marriages between people coming from the same part of the country account for 52 per cent of the total households). The matrimonial situation is also comparatively sound, as is shown in Table 3.

TABLE 3

MATRIMONIAL SITUATION IN BAMAKO
(100 people)
(*Etudes Démographiques* 1960:8)

	MEN		WOMEN			
Age	Bache-lors	Married	Spin-sters	Married	Widows	Di-vorced
15–19	100	–	23	76	–	1
20–24	83	17	3	94	1	2
25–29	51	49	1	94	2	3
30–34	21	79	1	96	2	1
35–39	14	86	1	91	3	5
40–49	19	91	–	77	16	7
50–59	13	87	–	47	49	4
60–69	13	87	–	38	60	2
70 & +	11	89	–	20	77	3
Average	39	61	5	83	9	3

Widows are numerous in comparison to the bush, and account for 9 per cent of the total female population. But divorced women make up only 3 per cent of the adult female population, and spinsters are all under thirty-nine years of age. It is possible that the random sample left out some unmarried women among the prostitutes, who are concentrated in three unsurveyed blocks. Their number probably does not exceed two hundred; most are foreigners (from Nigeria, Ghana, Niger, Ivory Coast, and Upper Volta). Actually prostitution is not yet a serious social problem, as it is not linked to procuring.

Because of the large number of married women, the gross rate of reproduction reaches 2.48 and the birth rate 60 per thousand, which is, as noted, as high as it is in the bush. Conversely, the rate of infant mortality is improbably low, fifty-eight per thousand. Better sanitary conditions and the growing resort to medical care by mothers may account for its being lower than in the country (180 per thousand) (*Etudes Démographiques* 1960:7, 11). The figures are questionable, and the statisticians also suspect some omissions. General mortality is low—sixteen per thousand. Here again, better hygiene and the comparatively small number of old people living in town may explain this figure. On the other hand, marriage is less stable than in the bush: half of the women between forty and forty-four have been married twice or more. The rate of polygyny is also lower, as Table 4 indicates. Seventy-one per cent of marriages are monogamous (against 65 per cent in other towns and 57 per cent in the rural areas). The polygyny average is 1.36. As is to be expected, the rate increases with the age of the husband.

The above data indicate that the population of Bamako is in many respects in better social health not only than the people in other African cities, but also, in some regards, than in the rural areas. Crimes are few: I heard of only one murder during the year I spent in town. Delinquency is rare: forty-three young men were indicted as juvenile delinquents in 1962 (Letter dated April 29, 1963, from the *Procureur de la République*). The commonest misdemeanors are thefts and petty crimes. Hence, police patrols are seen in the African sections only to pick up unlicensed bicycles. I did not find a single suicide recorded with the Ministry of Health.

TABLE 4

POLYGYNY IN BAMAKO
(100 people)
(*Etudes Démographiques* 1960)

Age-groups of the husband	One wife	Two wives	Three wives and more	Average number of wives
15–19	100	–	–	1.00
20–24	98	2	–	1.02
25–29	90	9	1	1.10
30–34	84	16	–	1.16
35–39	71	23	6	1.34
40–49	63	29	8	1.46
50–59	49	37	14	1.69
60–69	60	20	20	1.66
70 & +	65	17	18	1.58
Average	71	22	7	1.36

This social situation is quite noticeable as one walks along the streets: people are kind, and gladly answer your greetings. They are gay and witty, dress elegantly, and are prompt to put on entertainments at night in the street. As we shall see, this does not mean that social tensions are absent, but on the individual level the tensions do not seem to affect attitudes or social demeanor.

THE ECONOMIC ROLE OF BAMAKO

The administrative function of Bamako has been clearly shown through the history of the city. In order to examine the occupational structures of Bamako, it is necessary also to consider its economic functions.

The economic importance of Bamako was emphasized in 1955 in an official report on transportation in Mali: "To the classical disequilibrium of the 'Cercle,'[11] between the city and

[11] Mali is administratively divided into six *Régions*. The *Région de Bamako* is itself subdivided into eight *Cercles,* among which the *Cercle de Bamako* in 1962 was made up of 143 villages and 272,000 inhabitants, including the city of Bamako.

the country, is added a disequilibrium between the capital and other consuming centers of the territory, due to the administrative and technical centralization and to the concentration of profits and wages" (Tricard 1955:47). The author noted that, while the annual monetary income of Bamako dwellers was 12,500 francs [12] per capita, it was only 1,500 francs for the peasants living in the *Cercle*.

The geographical pattern of exchange has been considerably altered since 1960, following the breach of commercial relationships with Sénégal and the interruption of railroad traffic between the two countries. The economic importance of Bamako originally stemmed from the fact that it linked railroad traffic from Dakar and the sea with the Niger River traffic of the interior. Necessarily, Bamako became an important transit point and found itself at the intersection of two main axes: one between the Niger Bend and the sea and oriented from east to west, the other a north-south axis between Ivory Coast and Sénégal. Before the interruption of the Dakar-Niger Railroad, eastbound traffic was controlled by Dakar, which handled 93.4 per cent of the total Malian imports (excluding kola nuts) and 90.7 per cent of the exports (excluding fish and cattle). Of more than fifty-five thousand tons of imported goods from Sénégal that reached Bamako, twenty-three thousand tons were consumed in the city, eleven thousand went toward the eastern area (Ségou and Mopti), twenty-one hundred tons went to the neighboring areas (one thousand tons to Koulikoro, four hundred tons to Dioila and Fana, five hundred tons to Kolokani and Nara to the north, two hundred tons to Kangaba on the upper river), and nineteen thousand tons outside of Bamako *Cercle* to the rest of the country.

The east-west traffic was dominated by the commercial structure of the European trading concerns, which distributed the goods to local branches from their headquarters in Bamako. Actually, however, the southern towns and the area east

[12] At the time of the study, one Malian franc equaled two French centimes. One dollar equals 243 Malian francs. A devaluation of 50 per cent took place in 1967.

of Ségou were closer to Abidjan than to Dakar and would have been supplied more economically from Ivory Coast.[13]

While the eastbound traffic was largely under the control of the Europeans, the north-south trade was African. Bamako, as has been noted, had become one of the main markets for kola in West Africa: 16,500 tons of kola coming from Ivory Coast went through Bamako; 2,500 tons were consumed in the city; 700 tons went to the northern part of the country; 900 tons toward Koulikoro; 1,800 toward Ségou; 2,300 to the western part; and 8,000 tons were re-exported to Sénégal (Tricard 1955:157).

Recently there has been added a new north-south traffic in oil products, distributed by oil companies independent of the trading houses, and shipped from Abidjan largely by truck.

Most of the exports from Bamako went by rail toward Dakar: fourteen thousand tons of produce, of which peanuts accounted for eleven thousand tons. Less than one thousand tons were exported toward the Ivory Coast, Guinea (shea-butter), or Mopti and the Niger Bend (millet and rice).

With the breakup of the Mali Federation in 1960, the pattern of traffic was completely transformed. Abidjan became the main source of supplies, and the north-south traffic assumed overwhelming importance. A fleet of huge trucks were bought in Germany to compensate for the loss of rail facilities.[14] A report on transportation issued in 1962 (Irani 1962) gives the following figures: 25,000 tons of food, 16,000 tons of goods, and 38,500 tons of oil came from Ivory Coast. Of this total, sixteen thousand tons were re-exported to Ségou and Mopti (no figures are given for re-exportation to other areas).

Thus, the main consequence of the breakup of the Federation was that Bamako lost its central position as a distributing center. The southern part of the country, Mopti and all the downstream Niger Valley, could be supplied cheaply directly

---

[13] Abidjan made only 6.3 per cent of the total Malian imports and 7.7 per cent of the exports (kola, cattle, and fish excluded) (Tricard 1955).

[14] The road to Abidjan is asphalted for 430 kilometers (160 kilometers in Mali and 273 in Ivory Coast) out of a total distance of 1,300 kilometers.

from Abidjan without depending on Bamako. Part of the traffic was actually diverted to an east-southwest road, between Mopti and Ivory Coast, along the well-beaten path of the already existing fish traffic. Simultaneously, part of the kola trade, which could not reach Sénégal by train, went along the maritime road from Abidjan to Dakar. Imports of kola fell from 16,500 tons in 1959 to less than 6,500 tons in 1962.

This situation accounted for a business slump in Bamako while Mopti, directly geared to the rich markets of Ivory Coast and Ghana and less subject to customs controls, enjoyed a greater prosperity.

Discontent began to spread among the Bamako population, particularly among the merchants. Moreover, the economic eclipse of Bamako to the profit of eastern cities was not without political repercussions. These considerations, added to the fact that transportation by trucks and on dirt roads raised costs greatly, demonstrated that the break of relations with Sénégal had been an unfortunate move. Therefore, in June, 1963, relations were renewed, in time to prevent the downfall of Bamako's commercial and political dominance.

Traffic figures point to another feature of Bamako's economy: it is a consumer city. In 1955, the *Cercle de Bamako*[15] consumed 44.6 per cent of the imported oil products, 33 per cent of the cement, and 50 per cent of all other imported goods. Of 58,700 tons of products of all kinds imported into the *Cercle* through town, only 15,750 tons were re-exported to other parts of the country. The city of Bamako alone consumed twenty-three thousand tons.

The demand of the urban population has increased further during the last few years. From 1955 to 1962 food consumption grew by 8 per cent, imports of fabrics went up 4 per cent, and the distribution of electricity and water through public facilities rose by 50 per cent (Amin 1963). According to the national income figures (1959) (Comptes économiques 1962), African urban households—that is, for all cities over 2,500

---

[15] Figures are available only for the *Cercle* as a whole (Tricard 1955).

people—consumed an equivalent of 11,182 million francs, compared to 41,455 million francs for the rural population, or 21 per cent of the total Malian consumption. Since Bamako represents 44 per cent of the urban population, this would leave 9.3 per cent of the total national consumption for Bamako alone [16] (3 per cent of the total population).

In exchange Bamako provides scarcely any goods and manufactures very little. In fact, its main output, in a country where subsistence economy still accounts for 62 per cent of the national production, is cash income (salaries, wages, and profits).

The greatest number of wage earners in Mali are concentrated in the city of Bamako: 9,780, as against 9,203 for the rest of the country, or 54 per cent of the total wage earners.[17] Government employees in Bamako represent 45.5 per cent of the total, and among them are found nearly all the top executives and high-ranking officials. According to the national income figures (1959), the total amount of salaries and wages paid per year to African households throughout Mali is 8,717 million francs (*ibid.*:128), of which (we can assume on the basis of the above figures of employment) at least 50 per cent is distributed in Bamako—that is, the equivalent of 4,360 million francs. Another source of money income for the African households of Bamako is the profit from business. The national income figures give 5,740 million francs distributed to Malian entrepreneurs or shareholders (*ibid.*:112), of which one estimates that a third is distributed in Bamako.[18] Finally, one must count the wages and salaries paid to Europeans and spent in Bamako as an indirect source of income for African wage

[16] Actually, it is probably more, since the income level of the Bamako population is much higher than that in the smaller towns.

[17] Figures are from the National Labor Office. These figures are lower than those that can be computed from the 1960 partial census, which would give about fifteen thousand wage earners in Bamako. Actually, the Labor Office gives only the number of workers registered with them. Furthermore, there has been a sharp drop in employment since 1958, as a result of the closing up of several European enterprises. Comparison with 1958 figures of the Labor Office for the entire *Région* of Bamako shows a drop in the number of those employed in construction, transportation, and public services.

[18] The figure does not include exported profits.

earners and services. Of 4,101 millions paid (*ibid.*:128) to the Europeans in Mali, 1,829 millions are exported (*ibid.*:143), which leaves 2,272 millions to be spent within the country. It can be assumed that about 75 per cent of this amount is spent in Bamako, i.e., 1.7 billion.

If we add up these figures, we have the results shown in Table 5, which gives an approximation of the proportion of the nonexported cash income distributed in Bamako in relation to the rest of the country.[19] It can be seen that over 47 per cent of

TABLE 5

NONEXPORTED CASH INCOME
(in millions of Malian francs)

	Total Mali	Bamako	(estimates)
Wages and salaries paid to African households	8,717	4,360	(50%)
Wages and salaries paid to Europeans	2,272	1,700	(75%)
African business profits	5,740	1,900	(33%)
Total	16,729	7,960	

the total money income in Mali is distributed in Bamako. A great deal of this money is in turn re-exported to the rural area: in July, 1962, when the government changed the currency, only 14.81 per cent of the notes were collected in the city of Bamako (Banque de le Republique du Mali).

Bamako, therefore, exerts a triple attraction: as an administrative center employing a large number of government employees, as a place of business, and as a source of money income. The social and occupational structure of the town's population reflects this economic background (Tables 6 and 7).

BAMAKO SOCIETY: THE UPPER STRATA

Out of the administrative and commercial development of Bamako grew two "elite" groups: the civil servants and the

[19] The estimates have been made with the assistance of S. Amin, economist and author of the *Comptes économiques du Mali.*

TABLE 6

OCCUPATIONS OF MEN OVER FOURTEEN
(*Etudes Démographiques* 1960:11–12)

	Percentage of the group		Percentage of the subgroup	Percentage of the total
Agriculturists				10
Wage earners				42.5
Clerks	18.1			
Junior executives	15.9			
Workers	24.3			
mechanics			27	
brick layers			20	
carpenters			18	
smiths			6	
others			–	
Unskilled workers	22.1			
Employed for services	24.9			
chauffeurs			52	
servants			40	
others			–	
Salesmen	4			
Independents				36.1
Trade	50.2			
Craft	35.3			
textile			44.2	
wood			12.8	
leather			6.4	
metal			24.1	
Services	10.2			
chauffeurs & transporters			50.0	
Unemployed				4.1

merchants. The civil servants largely carried on the fight for independence, which expressed both their own aspiration toward self-government and the wishes of the workers' unions and peasantry for improvement of their living conditions, which had sharply deteriorated during the war and the period

TABLE 7

WAGE EARNERS, BAMAKO, DECEMBER 31, 1962

(République du Mali, Office national de la Main d'Oeuvre, Bamako)

Occupations	Execu- tives	Low Execu- tives	Clerks	Work- ers	Unskilled Laborers	Total
Agriculture	1	–	3	4	23	31
Building & road-works	5	29	62	480	503	1,079
Trade & banking	44	67	1,159	242	410	1,922
Manufacturing	3	23	1	616	442	1,085
Transportation	4	41	216	752	621	1,634
Professional	4	59	132	50	90	335
Servants	3	9	284	15	117	428
Civil servants	22	60	1,042	715	1,317	3,156
Total	86	288	2,899	2,874	3,523	9,670

of forced labor. Although compulsory labor had been abolished in 1946, fear of seeing such misery return was a great stimulus to support of the Union Soudanaise (U.S.).[20]

In contrast with the civil servants, the merchants were for the most part rich but illiterate, and hence unable to assume the task of governing a modern state. Though a few of them joined the U.S., most joined the *Parti Progressiste*, along with the traditional chiefs. After the victory of the U.S.–R.D.A., the civil servants took over the government. They had, however, no foothold in the economic structure of the country, and they endeavored to create a state economic sector through the partial nationalization of banking, transport, and public services. By so doing they pushed private business into more remote corners. Furthermore, in order to gain a closer control over the economy and remove the last French indenture, they raised customs duties, restricted external trade, and made the currency nonconvertible. These successive steps, added to the breach of relations with Sénégal, placed private business in a

[20] The Union Soudanaise was the Sudanese section of the Rassemblement Démocratique Africain (R.D.A.), a party fighting for independence in all French West Africa.

precarious position. In July, 1962, certain merchants and former members of the Progressiste party, supported by some foreign interests, vainly attempted to overthrow the government. Hundreds of merchants throughout the town were arrested and interrogated. A few of them went to trial and were condemned to jail. Nearly all were badly frightened. But though politically defeated, the Malian bourgeoisie is still a social force to take into account and a threat to the government.

The Civil Servants

At the time of the study (1963), the political power was in the hands of both the government and the party. The two organizations are closely linked: seven of the fifteen members of the government belong to the political bureau of the party, which is made up of nineteen members. Most of the government and the party officials are civil servants from the colonial period, educated in the French schools in Africa, either locally or in Dakar. Nearly all belong to a generation born between 1908 and 1918. They practice Islam and willingly wear sumptuous traditional garments. Among them the Manĩka, Bamana, and Fula people are the most numerous (see Table 8). The

TABLE 8

ETHNIC ORIGINS OF GOVERNMENT AND PARTY LEADERS

	Government	Party
Manĩka	4	7 + 2 *
Bamana	2	6 + 1
Fula	4	2 + 2
Songhai	1	2 + 1
Bozo	1	0
Dogõ	1	0
Toucouleur	1	0
Sonĩke	0	1
Unknown	1	1
	15	19

* Commissaires: high officials of the party who do not belong to the Bureau Politique.

dominance of western Mali is overwhelmingly represented by the Manīka and the Bamana. None belong to the traditional aristocratic order.

Following this first generation comes the younger one, men in their thirties, most of whom have a Parisian education. Half a dozen of them can already be found among the top echelon. But the great majority occupy second-level government positions (*Directeur de Cabinet, Chef de Cabinet, Conseillers techniques*) or are executives in state enterprises. In these positions, they work side by side with older men who lack education but have a record of militancy during the fight for independence. The ethnic composition of this group is slightly different from the top one. The Manīka make up the greatest number, followed by the Fula and the Sonīke, at the cost of the Bamana. Casted people and descendants from *wolo-so* (captives) are more numerous in these advisory positions.

Partly because of their social recruitment, but mostly because of their progressive convictions, they have less prejudice than their elders against intercaste or interclass marriages. They do not practice Islam as devotedly. Several have French wives. They live in European houses and dress in the European way—often in an elegant and sometimes in a conspicuous fashion. Their taste for beautiful cars and modern housing, their feelings of superiority from having been to the university in Paris, do not always make them popular among the people. However, they have contributed to setting new standards of living among the Bamako youth, who now firmly believe that no social success or occupational promotion can be achieved without a prolonged stay in France.

The development of the educational system in Mali and a tight control over exchanges, however, prevented many people in their twenties from attaining this goal. This new generation of young people with Malian education feel overwhelmed by their elders and slightly resentful toward them.

Such is the composition of the literate group from which bureaucratic recruits will come now and in the future. Among the three generations there is latent conflict. The men in power fear the rise of people with better educations than themselves. As more and more men return from foreign universities with fewer and fewer prestigious jobs to take, room must be made for them. The youngest generation may be frustrated if kept down by both older groups. Though these dissonances are still muffled, they are known and resented.[21]

The Merchants

The second major category in the Malian higher society consists of the merchants. Most of this group of African businessmen are involved in the African trade, partly inherited from the precolonial economy but largely resulting from the progress of transport and the general increase of purchasing power concomitant with the development of commercial agriculture. As we have mentioned before, most of these merchants are rich but illiterate. Their prosperity has been built within the African milieu and is separate from the European one.

Ethnically they belong to particular groups whose specialties are still sharply defined, though not, of course, absolute: the Sonīke, the Kokorogo, the Fula Jawābe, the Sikasso-kau, the Manīka-mory, and the Fula from Guinea.

The Sonīke are probably the most numerous, and they are found at all levels of trade. They come from Nioro, Kibun, and the Wagadu country. Others—called *marka-jalā* because they no longer speak Sonīke but have taken up Bamana—come from Niamina. The Sonīke are old-time migrants, both for wages and for business. They spread all over West Africa, even as far as the equatorial countries. They take advantage of their dispersal to create wide networks of commercial relationships covering several states and usually built on kinship or clientship links. They prefer to deal among themselves, as they distrust traders of other ethnic groups. The Sonīke have a reputation for fairness in business. Many of them have settled in Ivory Coast, where they constitute a rich and influential minority. Some hold official positions in the Ivorian adminis-

[21] A recent cabinet change (September, 1966) has wisely opened government positions to the "second generation."

tration; others are prominent businessmen in provincial towns such as Gagnoa. One of the richest Africans in the West is said to be a Malian diamond trader whose connections reach as far as Congo-Brazza and Congo-Léopoldville. He also owns several fine houses in the best sections of Bamako.

In the city, the Sonīke are known as traders in printed cloth. Because of their numerous connections with friends or kinsmen in Ivory Coast or Ghana, where many fashionable products originate, they are able quickly to offer the newest models on Bamako's market. Most of these traders learn their trade in Ivory Coast from a kinsman or a man from their village. After this apprenticeship they return to Bamako, where they work with another merchant of their acquaintance, who entrusts them with goods to peddle from door to door. Daily they bring the returns to their employer and share the profits with him, sometimes on an equal basis. The earnings of the apprentices are usually kept in the custody of the merchant until they are sufficient to enable the young man to enter in partnership with his "elder," or employer, either through the purchase of merchandise or by opening a small shop which is supplied with the senior partner's goods.

The Sonīke are also involved, in competition with the Moors, in trading in livestock. They buy their stock (cattle, sheep, or horses) in the Nara area, a traditional center of breeding in Sonīke country, and export it toward Ivory Coast, Ghana, and Liberia, or else supply the domestic market of Bamako through the butchers of Kati, an important slaughtering place eight miles from Bamako. A few of them are also interested in the kola business, but this trade is largely in the hands of another group, the Kokorogo.

The Kokorogo are a puzzling ethnic group, primarily concentrated in Wasululand in the southern part of the country, where they constitute a minority among sedentary and Bamanized Fula people. They prefer to marry among themselves, and they often take blacksmiths' or *griots'* surnames, although they do not belong to castes.

Kola trade is highly speculative and requires large circulating capital to face the wide price variations and the heavy losses that frequently arise from deterioration. For this reason, the trade is concentrated in the hands of a few men who have, besides capital, a flair for profitable deals and a skilled knowledge of how to handle this fragile and perishable good. Like the Sonīke, they deal through international networks spread from Ivory Coast, the main supplying market, to Sénégal, the major consuming country. They employ a comparatively large staff of people recruited among their kinsmen or close acquaintances. One can distinguish three ranks in the hierarchy of such enterprises: the owners and bosses are called *jula-ba* (great merchants), their associates at lower levels are said to be *jula-dē* (junior merchants) or *jula-kalādē* (merchant apprentices or pupils).

Some of the *jula-dē* are settled in the main producing centers of Ivory Coast where they buy and store the nuts. Other *dē* are stationed in the main towns of Ivory Coast and Sénégal, from which they cable, phone, or write the current selling or buying rates to Bamako. The goods are carried accordingly from the coast to Bamako by hired trucks and convoyed by the apprentices. In Bamako, the baskets are opened and the nuts are sorted into the various qualities, then mixed again according to complicated formulas. Then they are repacked and convoyed by rail by a *kalādē* to the various consuming centers, among which Dakar, Kaolack, and Kolda are the most important.[22] Profits and losses are shared by the *jula-ba* and their subordinates. Under these conditions, it is only through a succession of profitable operations that a *jula-kalādē* can earn enough money to participate in the purchase of goods and so become a *jula-dē* in partnership with a *jula-ba*.

Alongside this well-organized kola network, there is a parallel trade handled by Sonīke or unorganized Kokorogo, who buy the return freight from truck drivers coming from the coast. They sell mainly on the Bamako market. Often a *jula-ba* turns

---

[22] During the break in the railroad traffic, most of the nuts went from Abidjan to Dakar by boat; the trade remained, for the most part, in the hands of the same networks.

over part of his own cargo to unorganized Kokorogo, in the spirit of mutual aid which is common among these people.

The real Jula are the people from Sikasso, a town in the southeastern part of the country. They are much like the Kokorogo people in appearance, and they are easily mistaken for Kokorogo, since they too engage in the kola trade. They also transport dried fish and cattle from Mopti to the coast countries.

The last important group of tradesmen are of Guinean origin: the *Manīka-mori.* They deal in nearly all kinds of goods—cloth, grains, manufactured goods, and also kola— though they have a reputation for being very cautious in this trade (they are nicknamed *sigi-sigila ka,* hesitating people). They are numerous in Bamako and dwell in the section of Bamako Coura; their shops are in Bozola, the African section nearest to the central market. Though well-to-do, none of them are known to be as wealthy as the Kokorogo or the Sonīke. The *Jalōke-Fula,* from Fouta-Djalon in Guinea, are traders and carriers, bringing fruits from Guinea and taking back shea-butter, which is in high demand on the Guinean market.

All together, these merchants form a kind of native bourgeoisie of African stock and culture. They work in an almost exclusively African milieu, providing an African market with African goods. They dress in a traditional manner, often sumptuously. Their cultural model is not European but Arabian. Religiously they are devout Moslems. Most of the richest among them have gone to Mecca on one or more pilgrimages, and proudly wear the title of El Hadj. Many Kokorogo belong to the Wahabite sect, which is very unpopular among the other Moslems of Bamako, most of whom are Quadrya or Tidjanist. Indeed, a few years ago they were the object of a near pogrom. Wahabism is dominant in Mecca, and after the war the rich merchants were the first to undertake a holy pilgrimage there and bring back the new rite to Bamako. But they adopted it for very practical reasons. Their illiteracy was a growing hindrance as business became increasingly complex and as more paper work was required for administrative purposes. However, these traditional merchants were reluctant to send their children to the public school, which was nondenominational and dominated by Europeans. They preferred a religious education, but the old-fashioned Koranic school of the Quadrya or the Tidjanist did not teach anything but the psalmody of Arabic letters. The Wahabites, on the other hand, inaugurated in Bamako a more modern system of education. In their *medersa* (from the Arabic, school) Arabic and French are taught concurrently, along with all the other subjects, on the model of the European school, but dominated by Islam.

Thus, the two leading social and economic groups, the civil servants and the merchants, are highly dissimilar. One is educated, the other illiterate. One is devoted to clerical, administrative, and political functions; the other is committed to trade. One is European minded; the other is Arab oriented. One is tolerantly religious (with a tendency to atheism among the younger generation); the other is bigoted.

Economically, they are antagonistic and competitive. In their search for profits, the merchants yearn for freedom of business, while the civil servants, as representatives of collective interests, impose more and more controls. In their position as entrepreneurs, the merchants are employers and providers of funds for a long line of patrons. Concurrently, because government representatives manage the state as a corporate business, the civil servants provide contracts and deals to businessmen and wages and salaries to a great number of wage earners. Individually, the civil servants carry a great economic burden. These officials should, in theory, have no personal income other than their salaries, which range from 100,000 to 140,000 francs a month. In fact, they also have "fringe benefits" as a result of their official positions, such as the use of a car and the occupancy of a modern house. Furthermore, a highly criticized tendency toward individual business profit is creeping in. Indeed, businessmen are not totally excluded from the government; some of the officials are prosperous businessmen. They tend to set a standard of wealth among their equals. Taking advantage of their influential position, a few officials are acquiring capitalistic positions by purchasing and renting out houses—usually bought through the good offices and even in the name of merchants, or through participation in private enterprises.

Could the two groups eventually become amalgamated? After the attempted coup of July, 1962, the merchants considered themselves politically defeated; their main concern was to demonstrate their loyalty to the regime. They assiduously attended party meetings and contributed generously and obviously to various national subscriptions. Still, their position is ambiguous and contradictory: they believe that their economic function should give them more weight in politics, but their conservative education bars them from the executive ranks. If some merchants believe it to be good politics to accept government people into their trade, others regard it as a dangerous move, considering the influential position of their new competitors. Nevertheless, under the threat of the new generation of educated young men, some older politicians, after having gained control of private economic positions, sought support from the native bourgeoisie in order to stay in power, but this move was contradicted in 1968 by the "Cultural Revolution."

BAMAKO SOCIETY: THE LOWER STRATA

The two leading groups, being the providers of employment and money, shape the remainder of the population to their own image, along two parallel social lines—one in accordance with the traditional economic relationships (the apprentices and mates), the other grounded on a more modern contractual basis (the wage earners). In addition there are the petty traders, craftsmen, and personal servants, who live according to the customs of the upper strata, and the "clients," whose culture is inherited from the ancient society.

The Wage Earners

The wage earners make up the largest single group of active people in Bamako: 42.5 per cent of all adult men, as against

36.1 per cent of the so-called "independents."[23] Although statistics are not available, it is evident that the government and private European business are the largest employers of wage earners. In the hierarchy of wage earners, the executives in government agencies and in commercial enterprises fall just below the top officials described above. They earn from forty thousand to eighty thousand francs a month. Socially they belong to what could be called the modern middle class, eager to reach a higher social level, but still kept out of the new elite group of the high administration. They do not benefit from advantages in kind to the same extent as do their superiors.[24]

Next come the greatest bulk of government workers, earning a monthly salary of eight thousand to thirty thousand francs, although most of them receive between ten thousand and fifteen thousand. This group was the first to enjoy social benefits in addition to salaries. Since August, 1962, family allowances and health and pension plans have been extended to all wage earners. In private business, the best-paid African wage earners are the clerks employed in European enterprises. Although they sometimes earn over thirty-five thousand francs a month, most earn between ten thousand and fourteen thousand. The skilled workers' wages average twelve thousand francs, and range from ten thousand to fifteen thousand francs. Among them, the chauffeurs are comparatively well paid— between twelve thousand and seventeen thousand francs. Unskilled workers average about six thousand francs, while manual laborers' wages vary widely between four thousand and five thousand francs up to ten thousand and even twelve thousand. Finally, servants earn from five thousand to eight thousand, when employed by Europeans or by Europeanized Africans.[25]

---

[23] Here we consider as wage earners people employed permanently under contract and paid by an hourly, weekly, or monthly wage.

[24] In 1963, the government decided that the use of administrative cars shall be denied officials below the rank of *Directeur de Cabinet,* which is that directly below the rank of Minister.

[25] This material has been gathered from questionnaires distributed in the census of 1960.

The Apprenctices and Mates

Another appendage to traditional African business involves a different type of relationship at work. As we have seen in the case of the kola trade, there is little difference between partnership and employment. Furthermore, to be employed by an African usually involves some links of a personal nature, either familial or neighborly. The employee is in the personal custody of his master, whose duties toward him go beyond the mere paying of wages. The master must teach his trade to his apprentice or pupil, must often provide his room and board, and must help him in case of need. He is also obliged to settle the young man in business, and for that purpose he usually keeps his *kalãdẽ*'s earnings in custody in order to invest them, with some of his own money, in a new trade. A *kalãdẽ*'s income is difficult to estimate, since he does not receive wages proper. Beyond a little cash for personal expenses, this income is made up of returns and profits, plus noncomputable advantages in kind.

The Smaller Traders

In addition to the wage earners, the statisticians distinguish another group—the "independents," who participate for the most part in the African trades and businesses, but whose income and standards vary so widely that it is difficult to regard them as a single social category. We have already described the high-ranking group among them. Below this group, we meet lesser businessmen—certified traders owning small shops, such as grocers, soft-drink salesmen, bakers, and so forth. They have some relationship with the rich merchants, from whom they often borrow money. Many of them suffered greatly from the new policy of government business restrictions, following Independence.

The next important group and the largest numerically, is composed of small traders, craftsmen, and people providing services who live off the patronage of the profit makers and wage earners. Among the small traders, the butchers seem to have the highest income (about twelve thousand francs a month).[26] Next come the innumerable petty traders and peddlers selling trinkets, sugar, cigarettes, candies, and the like on street corners. Their capital usually comes from an elder or an acquaintance, and they live partly from their profits. They practice trading in the expectation of finding a better job. Their incomes are difficult to estimate, since they usually fail to distinguish their business and personal expenses. I estimate that their gain varies from fifteen hundred to three or four thousand francs a month. Although a few of them declare as much as eight or nine thousand, that would seem to be an attempt at prestige through false reporting.

Modern craftsmen—such as tailors, mechanics, cabinetmakers, painters, bricklayers, plumbers, mattress makers—earn from three thousand to thirteen thousand francs a month. Among this group, the jewelers are probably the most successful, but we have no estimates of their income. Leather workers making cases for Koranic verses or objects for sale to the tourists get a return of between three thousand and five thousand francs. One must also mention the woodworkers and the ironsmiths manufacturing various domestic objects out of scrap iron—trunks, stove pans, and the like—which they sell to intermediaries. Finally, we find the weavers, who do not always work for themselves. Often they weave for women who provide them with thread and pay them between six hundred and twelve hundred francs for each piece of *pagne* (cloth), depending on the pattern.

Services are performed by laundrymen, who collect laundry from door to door to wash in the river; by barbers standing near a chair and table in the street or on public squares; shepherds, who come daily to take the sheep from their customers' wards to the fields, and so forth. The list of these activities is long, and the above are only a few examples of the diversity brought about by the new economy of specialization.

Perhaps the marabouts and beggars should be added to

[26] We collected these data about income returns as above, since some profit makers also answered this questionnaire.

this group that lives off the wage earners. The professional marabouts [27] act as Koranic teachers and advisers. They are consulted on various domestic or personal affairs, and they practice divination or act as intercessors with Allah, but only if they receive recompense, sometimes in considerable amounts. According to Islamic tradition, Koranic teachers receive gifts from their neighbors and from the parents of their pupils. The city, which is almost totally Islamized, is a favorable milieu for a marabout's activities. Cases are reported of swindles perpetrated by fake marabouts.

For the same religious reasons, one finds in Bamako a great number of beggars, who go from ward to ward alone or in groups, singing religious verses and receiving food. They are usually invalid, blind, maimed, or sick (though lepers do not usually beg in the African wards). Beggars do not originate from mere misery. There are no beggars in the bush where these people come from. They are the by-product of Islam.

The Clients

The clients are not an important group numerically, but they still play a noticeable social role. They are the *ñamakala* (casted people), the most important among them being the *jeli*, the *fune*, or members of other castes who have traditionally been dependent on noble families. Their functions are to act as factotums, *porte-paroles*, and intermediaries between families and people. They are also musicians, bards, and entertainers. No marriage can take place without their active participation. Ceremonies are unthinkable without the *ñamakala* acting as heralds, musicians, and dancers in exchange for gifts and money. On the occasion of all public celebrations or holidays, *ñamakala* women come to visit their "customers" to sing their praises and receive gifts. Today many *ñamakala* by birth have jobs and have given up their ancient functions; the few who

---

[27] They should be distinguished from the *imam* or other men of the cult who belong to the city's secular community, work at their own trades, and receive gifts from their parishioners as a means of maintaining their mosques.

still act according to their former status—although learned in
the tradition—are usually illiterate, scarcely speak French,
dress in the African way, and devotedly practice the Islamic
religion.

The Seasonal Workers

To the permanent population of Bamako, one must add a
floating population, estimated at ten or fifteen thousand people,
who come from the bush during the dry season to earn cash in
order to pay the family taxes or buy cloth. For the most part
they are young men between fifteen and thirty. They come by
passenger trucks from Nioro, Nara, and Banamba in the Sonīke areas, and to a lesser extent from the country around
Ségou, Bougouni, and San. They stay in town for as long as six
months, from December to July. They usually take shelter
with a kinsman or with a man from their village, whom they
sometimes know only by repute. Often they return year after
year to the same ward, even though their original host has gone
away. They sleep in the *blõ* (the cabin standing at the entrance
of the ward), and their host supplies part of their daily meals.
In exchange they work for him on Sundays at building, cleaning, or carrying. Others join together to rent a room, and either
take their meals with a family to whom they pay a small
amount of money or buy prepared foods in the market. During
the day they wander around the streets, expecting to be called
upon to perform all kinds of manual work: carrying, building,
brickmaking, ditchdigging, and the like. They are paid at the
rate of twenty-five to fifty francs an hour, or by piece rate:
twenty-five to fifty francs to carry a load of kola across town,
or two to three francs each for making bricks. On the average
they may earn two hundred to four hundred francs a day, and
some return home with thirty thousand francs after six months
in town. Many seasonal workers from the Bougouni area bring
their wives, who work as servants in African families. They
receive food for themselves and their husbands, plus a monthly
wage of 250 to 300 francs. These categories of workers, the

bara-ñini (*bara*, work; *ñini*, to seek), are among the lowest paid and, since they are not officially registered, do not benefit from social security.

As the above analyses show, it is difficult to make clear distinctions among the social classes. Indeed, people still belong to various social milieus, old and new, which interpenetrate. Family links and old ties from the country villages are very strong. One finds within the same family or the same friendly group, wage earners, craftsmen, high officials, rich businessmen, and manual laborers. On the other hand, ancient forms of relationships are maintained between *horō* (noble people) and casted people, or between them and *wolo-so* (slave descendants), so that even if the latter occupy a high rank in business or in government, they depend at home on an old man, a former *commis* or *planton* without an education. Finally, as we have noted, work and business relationships belong to two different systems. In the African sector, they remain firmly embedded in personal relationships of a paternalistic kind, sometimes even inherited from the servile system. But it is the wage earning group that is, after all, the most modern in its social reactions to labor problems. While the "patrons" look to their employer or lender for security, as to an elder and protector, the wage earners act through organized labor unions.

CHAPTER TWO

The Cultural Background

THE ETHNIC GROUPS

THE social organization of city people owes something to the traditional way of life and something to conformity with modern social patterns. An exact appraisal of both influences requires a good knowledge of the cultural background as well as an understanding of modern conditions of life. Unfortunately, the anthropological literature on the main populations found in the city is still inadequate, and what exists is for the most part not related to social organization. On the basis of available studies and of information gathered in the field, we shall describe briefly the social traits of the most numerous ethnic groups.

The statistical census of Bamako shows that four ethnic groups—Bamana, Manīka, Fula, and Sonīke—make up 67 per cent of the total population. Of the remainder, no single one accounts for as much as 10 per cent of the population, so only the four major groups will be described here.

The Bamana (Bambara)

The Bamana are the most numerous single ethnic group in Bamako, as they are in Mali. Their capacity for assimilation is impressive, and the Bamana dialect has become (with the help

of the French army) a lingua franca throughout much of West
Africa.

The word "Bamana" is applied to a population whose ethnic
and physical characteristics are highly diversified. More than a
tribe, it designates a people historically formed from several
ethnic groups (Monteil 1924). According to the records left by
Arabian writers, the Bamana were the agricultural, pagan, and
dark-skinned peoples. The Bamana are peasants, who settled
in the open, fertile plain south of the Sahel, along the upper-
middle Niger. Formerly, this area was subject to slave raids,
and the Bamana peasants were compelled to take up arms and
become warriors, either to protect themselves or to participate
in looting. Military clans divided the country into small chief-
doms; huge and strong fortifications were erected around the
villages, and mounted soldiers, the *sofa* (*so,* horse), were
trained. With the rise of the kingdom of Ségou in the eight-
eenth century, the Bamana came to be dreaded as fierce warriors.

For the Bamana people, agriculture is still the noblest endeavor. However, in spite of the fact that they themselves did
not trade, their chiefs and sovereigns welcomed the Moorish
merchants and gladly dealt with them. They also welcomed the
Islamic marabouts, who were consulted as the equal of other
wizards. But since they built their strength against the pressure of Islamized people (among them the Peul of Macina),
they have remained stubbornly pagan until recent years.

As is indicated by such examples as Ségou and other towns,
the Bamana were not completely devoid of an urban tradition.
Still, their usual dwelling places were villages of three hundred
to one thousand people, surrounded by a *tata*. They built
square, flat, earthen-roofed houses and therefore were well
protected against fire. Behind the *tata,* each domestic unit lived
within its own *ji,* a wall surrounding the *du,* or group of houses
circling a central yard called *du-kene.*

The Bamana people are divided into clans, each claiming a
common ancestor, but today they are often scattered and subdivided into lineages whose common origin is sometimes ob-

scure. The clans are patronymic: all members of the same clan bear the same patronym or *jamu*. This trait is found throughout the area from Sénégal to the Hausa country, and therefore in the four groups we are considering, but the *jamu* is not found either to the north among the Moorish or Berber populations, or to the south among the forest people. The clan members respect a *tana:* some animal, food, or even action prohibited to them. People carrying the same *jamu* and respecting the same *tana* should not marry.

The social organization is patrilineal, patrilocal, and polygynous. The actual living social cell is the *gwa,* formed around a lineage or the fragment of a clan and made up of all the people, kinsmen, clients, servants, and slaves living together in the same *du* and consuming the same food. Such *gwa* are headed by the eldest male of the lineage. A village is formed by several *gwa,* under the head of the most influential *gwa,* who is sometimes from a warrior clan.

On a more general level, Bamana society is divided into three main categories: the *horõ,* the *ñamakala,* and the *jõ.* The title of *horõ* belongs to anyone of free condition who is not from a caste and who has never come under submission through capture or purchase. They are the aristocratic or noble group. The *horõ* are proud of their status and uphold a code of values that distinguishes them from the other social groups. A *horõ* should be brave, humble, modest, and loyal. He must also act as the natural protector and patron of the caste and slave people. Though their main occupation is agriculture (the most honorable one), *horõ* people are also the civilian or military leaders of the largest communities—villages or seigniories.

The *ñamakala* are the people of castes. A caste is composed of clans, with the usual characteristics: common origin, *jamu,* and *tana.* It is also associated with a craft or a function. Only the *ñamakala* may practice the craft which is their own, but they are not compelled to do so. Though it is their specialty, it is not a specialization since they also cultivate the land. *Horõ* people cannot marry *ñamakala.* This prohibition is still respected today in all circles despite the official ideology condemning social discrimination. There are several castes, and they exist among other peoples living next to the Bamana or among them. Thus there is some uncertainty as to which castes are authentically Bamana.

The *numu* or blacksmiths are the most respected, and are considered to be magicians. Legends describe them as an aboriginal population found on the spot by newcomers. Historically, the blacksmiths in this area knew how to extract metal from iron ore. They also made and repaired guns. Their wives are potters. In each village where they settle, they are closely associated with social and political decisions.

The next caste is the *jeli* (*griots*), who are bards, musicians, and genealogists, often used as factotums and intermediaries by the *horõ* in courtship, marriage, and, formerly, in diplomacy among themselves. The *jeli* were often counselors to the sovereigns. They live on gifts from the *horõ* and are not ashamed to ask for them. For this reason they are considered as inferior by the *horõ*, but are also dreaded for their sharp tongues and their reputations of slandering whoever is not generous enough with them.

The *jõ* form the lowest stratum.[1] They were originally *horõ* people taken in war or sold by their kinsmen. The *ñamakala* could not be enslaved. If they were captured in war, they had a right to make themselves known as *ñamakala* and be freed. Uncircumcised children of a defeated lord were not enslaved either, but adopted and brought up among the children of the victor. The status of the slaves varied with their generation. The people taken in war or purchased were *jõ* proper. Among them, women and children were the most numerous, since men were usually killed. A *jõ* was not a man to be fully trusted because, being of noble descent, his moral duty was to try to escape and recover his freedom. He could also be freed through repurchase: his status was not yet irreversible. The male *jõ* could not marry *horõ* women, but a *horõ* man could take a

[1] Slavery has been abolished. However, people of slave descent still are considered, for the most part, as socially inferior. Marriages between a *horõ* woman and a man of slave descent are uncommon.

jõ-muso as a wife or concubine (not the first, but only as the fifth or subsequent one). If she bore children, she and her child were freed. Otherwise *jõ* people married one another. Their offspring were called *wolo-so.* They were educated with their master's children, but with full understanding of their inferior position. A *wolo-so* could not be freed by either escape or repurchase. He lived among his masters as a perpetual dependent. The *horõ* claimed that *wolo-so* had an inferior moral code. Though they could be trusted better than *horõ* in some private affairs or as confidants, they lacked the *horõ*'s moral obligation not to lie or steal. Furthermore, they were insolent and immodest and traditionally acted as buffoons.

Slaves of the subsequent generation are often confused with the *wolo-so,* but actually the descendants of the *wolo-so* were called *tibrigeñe,* and their ties with their masters were eased off, except for a few living among the family. Slaves from the fourth generation and beyond were called *jõ-ba* (great slaves) or *foro-ba jõ* (community or common slaves).[2] They did not belong to one master in particular, but to the community at large. Some lived in their own villages under a headman chosen among themselves; they worked four days a week for the community and three days a year for its head in order to maintain the *tata* and the *muniã* (residence of the chief). In case of war, they fought side by side with the other villagers against the common enemy; they traded on behalf of the chief, and they were allowed to keep slaves of their own—the *jõ-ba jõ* (slaves of the great slaves). Still, they could not marry *horõ* people, and there is no end, theoretically, to this prohibition.

The Sonike (Sarakole)

The oldest population with a historical tradition are the Sonike. Yet they have not been adequately studied. We have only a few old monographs about localized populations; we know only a few legends about their origins and a few accounts

---

[2] *Foro,* field; *ba,* great; *foro-ba,* the great field cultivated in common by people of a same *gwa.* Therefore this locution has become the equivalent of "common."

from Arab travelers about their history. The Sonīke were the subjects of the ancient empire known as Ghana (locally called Wagadu), with the great city of Kumbi-Saleh as one of its capitals. Legend says that twenty-two kings reigned before the hegira and twenty-two afterward, but there is no other information about the pre-hegira period. Wagadu became a prosperous country, exploiting gold from the Bure and benefiting from the trade between the Maghreb and the Sudanese area. However, from the eighth century (or before) to the thirteenth, this empire suffered in succession a great drought, destruction by the Almoravides (eleventh century), and the final attack by the Manīka kingdom of Mali (thirteenth century). Each of these events seems to have been the beginning of a new dispersal of the Sonīke populations, which can be found today from Nioro to San on the Bani River (Delafosee 1912; El Bekri 1965; Monteil 1953; Saint-Père 1925). They probably carried with them many customs that were adopted by their hosts, and therefore their social and historical importance has no doubt been underestimated. An old tradition claims that a Sonīke king reigned over the Ségou area before Sundiata's time. Sonīke are said to have founded the cities of Dia, Djenne, and Sāsani (Sansanding). Some Bozo are said to be of Sonīke origin. As we have seen, the leading clan of Bamako, the Niaré, is also Sonīke.

Today, the Sonīke are well-known as traders throughout West and Equatorial Africa. The poorest of them made up the bulk of the *navetanes,* or migrant workers who, before the breakup of the Mali Federation, went to Sénégal to work as migrant laborers at peanut-cropping time. Today, these migrant workers go to France, and more than twenty thousand of them are looking for jobs in Paris.

The Sonīke are nearly all Moslems. They are patrilineal, patrilocal, and polygynous. The lineage seems to be firmly held in hand by the elders; its compactness is maintained through preferential marriage between parallel cousins. In addition there is a crisscrossing of adoptive relationships between father's brother and brother's son, father's sister and brother's

daughter, co-wives and each other's children. Otherwise their
social features are similar to those of the Bamana. Like the
latter, their society is divided between *horō* (nobles), *ñaxamala*
(caste people), and *komo* (slaves). In addition to the *tage*
(blacksmiths), and the *jare* or *gesere* (*griot*), who have similar functions, one finds the *garāke*, or leather workers, whose
women sometimes specialize in beauty treatment (darkening of
the gums or hairdressing). Again, as with the Bamana, the
slaves are subdivided into several classes, according to the
number of generations that have elapsed since their original
capture or purchase.

The Manīka (Mandinka, Malīke)

The Manīka are best known through the history of Sūjatta,
founder of the empire of Mali. They settled, originally, in the
upper Niger Valley, a hilly country comparatively well protected. Today, they spread from the upper Sénégal Valley in
the north as far south as the border of the forest. Their villages
were fortified, but not as strongly as were those of the Bamana.
Their houses were roofed with thatch, easy to set afire. Though
their chronicles and traditions mention former capitals of great
renown, no trace has yet been found of any large city.[3] History
recalls that the Manīka fought a long time against Sumaoro,
lord of Sosso (not to be confused with the Susu country) and
former vassal of the king of Wagadu. They fought later against
the Jolof and destroyed the remains of the Wagadu empire.
Sixteen clans are said to have formed the original federation
that defeated Sumaoro under the leadership of Sūjatta Keita.
Together with five other maraboutic clans, they constitute the
aristocracy of the Manīka people (Delafosse 1912; Dieterlen
1955; Monteil 1930; Mauny 1959 and 1961).

The social organization is nearly identical, as far as we
know, with that of the Bamana. The castes are the blacksmiths
(*numu*), the griot (*jeli* and *fune*), and probably the *gawlo*

[3] Reports from the Republic of Guinea state that Niani, one ancient headtown
of Mali, has been found by Guinean and Polish archaeologists (1965).

(who might be of foreign origin—wizards, healers, and traders) (Leynaud 1961; Labouret 1934).

The Fula

The Fula people spread from Sénégal to the Hausa country. Their mores and customs vary from one group to another. In the area with which we are concerned, their most commonly recognized characteristics are that they all speak Fulfulbe, they are cattle breeders, and they have light-colored skins, so that they are often referred to as "whites" or *fara-je* by the other peoples. All Fula are said to belong to four original clans, but the nomadic life has, according to Tauxier (1937), insured against the formation of large units. The three social categories are the *rimbe* or noble, the *jemube* or caste people, and the *rimaibe* or slaves. The castes are the *wailbe* (blacksmiths), the *laobe* (woodworkers), the *sake* (leather workers), the *mabube* (weavers), and the *bambabe* (bards).

The main group of Fula in Mali are the Macina people who were half sedentarized and completely Islamized by Amadu Sheikou in the first half of the nineteenth century. This holy man, accredited as a Sheik by Usman dan Fodio from Bornu, freed the Fula from the kingdom of Ségou. He organized the new empire administratively and militarily, regulated and protected the movements of the cattle, and erected cities of impressive stature (A. H. Ba and J. Daget 1962; Tauxier 1937). Besides the Fula from Macina, who live together in a continuous area, many families are scattered among the Bamana, Manīka, or Sonīke villages; they live in small settlements, trading milk for millet or herding their neighbors' cattle. Many of these families have adopted the local dialect and customs. Some large groups, such as the people from Wasulu in the south of Bamako, are today sedentary agriculturists, speak Bamana, and are animists.

The above data show that the four peoples described have a great many social traits and institutions in common. They all bear patronymic clan surnames, they all are divided into noble, caste, and slave people. They all are patrilineal, patrilocal, and polygynous. They have been in constant contact either through war or through alliances. They often live intermingled, and several clans are said to belong to more than a single tribe. The castes are spread among the various peoples, and in spite of their different ethnic backgrounds, a hierarchy exists among them. Many secondary peoples, such as the Kasōke and the Dialōke (Fula), the Kagoro (Manīka), the Miniāka (Bamana), are closely related to one or another of the above, and have similar social structures. The Songhai from the Niger Bend and their associated populations are also organized along the same line, the differences being largely cultural, religious, and historical.

Among the peoples described above, various clans from different origins often live together in the same villages. Hence, intermarriages, matrimonial alliances, and blood brotherhood are not uncommon among them. The intermingling of these various peoples is not a new phenomenon; it does not raise tribal conflicts, and it is not a major factor in regrouping the inhabitants within the city.

THE TRADITIONAL ASSOCIATIONS

The grouping of people into many sorts of associations is part of the traditional way of living among the peoples mentioned above. Here again, we should describe the associations of all four of them, but unfortunately information is even more scarce on this subject than on others, and most of what we know concerns the Bamana and the Manīka. We shall refer here primarily to the Bamana institutions and shall use the terminology of the Bamana vernacular.[4]

Like kinship, the *tō* (rule or association) is a prominent principle of Bamana social organization. The word *"tō,"* however, does not cover a single type of association. Its meaning is indeed no more precise than our word "association." Roughly, a *tō* is a group of people from the same village or neighborhood, selected according to a common characteristic (age, be-

[4] Most of the description comes from information gathered from elder men in Bamako.

lief, activity), who submit to a certain number of rules and organize themselves hierarchically. The concept of *tõ* also embodies an idea of collective discussion, and the word applies to any group of people gathered in a formal assembly. Properly speaking, a family or a clan is not a *tõ*, though it will be when the members are sitting together to debate under the aegis of an elder. A king's court is not a *tõ* except when gathered in a formal meeting. When people gather informally, the Bamana refer to such an assembly as a *grẽ*.

The meaning that interests us here is associated with a permanent type of association, which remains a *tõ* whether it is in session or not. Such a *tõ* is like a fictional person standing over its members, so that loyalty is due to the *tõ* rather than to its leaders. Examples are the *flã-tõ* (*fila*, two; *flã*, twin), or organized age-sets; the *senene-tõ* (*senene*, to cultivate), or permanent work group; the *dõso-tõ*, or hunters' association; and, formerly, the *tegere-tõ* or *kele-tõ* (*tegere*, bandit; *kele*, war), warriors gathered into organized bands. In its widest meaning, one can also consider the village a *tõ* (*dugu-tõ*) (*dugu*, village or settlement).

Young People's Associations

It is repeatedly stated that, in former times, circumcision took place late in the youth of the individual, as a gateway to adulthood and marriage. Until then the boys were called *bila-koro* (wearers of drawers—*bila*, drawers; *koro*, to wear). They were organized into work groups, the *senene-tõ*, cultivating the fields of the needy families of the village. Belonging to this *tõ* was considered to be an essential part of a young man's education. The *senene-tõ* was led by the oldest *bila-koro* and supervised by adults, called the *tõ-fa* or the *tõ-ba* (*fa*, father; *ba*, mother) who were usually people of caste or *wolo-so*. Their main function was to instruct *tõ* members about general social rules and to keep the *tõ* within its limitations.

The age of circumcision has been progressively lowered, until the operation is now performed when a young person is under fifteen, and sometimes no more than eight years old. The village organization of the *flã-tõ* has been consequently altered, and is today as follows.

Each propitious year—they occur sporadically—the young boys and girls of the correct age (between eight and fifteen) and of all social conditions are circumcised or excised at the same time, though the sexes are separated. They belong thereafter to the same *flã-bolo* (*bolo*, hand), one for each sex. All *flã-bolo* of the same sex are gathered into a single village *flã-tõ*, one for the boys and one for the girls. The eldest in the *flã-tõ* will be men newly married or with very small children. Each *flã-bolo* has its own leader (*flã-tie tigi* for the boys and *flã-muso tigi* for the girls), in theory, the eldest of the set or, in case of incapacity or refusal, anyone drawn by lot. The *flã-tõ* is responsible to a leader, chosen according to the same rules. The men's *flã-tõ* carries more weight than the women's for the simple reason that it lasts longer, since women marry earlier than men. Until marriage, intimate relationships are created between boys and girls of corresponding *flã-bolo*. They are usually coupled by the *flã-tigi* in a kind of conjugal union which excludes sexual intercourse. The girl will undertake for her *flã-tie* such domestic work as washing, cleaning, and eventually cooking and bringing food to him while at work. In return, the boy is responsible for the sexual behavior of his partner, who must remain virgin until marriage. Should she not so remain, her young guardian is blamed and punished (whipped).

The *flã-tõ* has two main functions in the village: collective work and entertainment. On Fridays (which have become days of rest under Islamic influence) the young vigorous men from the *tõ* work in turn in the fields of each head of a family in the village, or even in neighboring ones. The *tõ* undertakes other collective tasks, of interest to the community at large, while one of the young men wears the *cywara* mask to stimulate them. In each case, the *tõ* receives choice food, gifts, and a small share of the crop. These goods are the common property of the *tõ*, and the older people have no right to them. They are used either for private celebrations, usually with the participation of the girls' *tõ,* or for celebrating the wedding of a member. Girls do various work, such as ginning, spinning, or hairdressing, to collect gifts and money for their *tõ.*

Entertainment is largely the business of boys from the *flã-tõ.* They organize dances, and they also perform, in some Bamana and Manĩka areas, a farcical and satirical theater called the *Koteba* (Meillassoux 1965).

The activities of the *flã-tõ* are debated during sessions in which all the *flã* are gathered. These debates are called *tõ-sigi* (*sigi,* to seat). As in any other *tõ,* these meetings are democratic, but controlled by strict rules and discipline. No one is allowed to gossip during the session, under penalty of fine. No one may take the floor without asking, but everyone is invited to express his opinion. Only one person at a time may speak, and this is always done through a *dalamina* (*da,* mouth; *la,* in; *mine,* to take), usually a man of caste who repeats aloud the words of the speaker, sentence by sentence. *Tõ-sigi* are frequent, sometimes taking place every day.

Old Men's Associations

Besides the youth, the old men also have their own permanent assembly, the *fere* (public square). Each family head in turn invites the others to his *du-kene,* or to any other place away from the ears of younger people, to debate village affairs or talk about personal matters. The *fere* does not have such strict rules as the youngsters' *tõ,* due to the maturity and responsibility of its members. It is the heart of village political life.

Esoteric Societies

The village is also dominated by esoteric and initiatory societies which are considered by many authors to be of religious significance. There are five of these societies in Bamana country, which are, according to Zahan (1960), the five steps toward a deeper religious knowledge. Unfortunately, Zahan's studies are metaphysical interpretations of esoteric, symbolic, and cosmological aspects of these associations and are not related to their social content and functions. According to our own sparse information, three of these societies are widespread in Bamana country: the *n'tomo,* the *komo,* and the *nama.* The other two, the *kore* and the *kono,* are found in fewer villages.

The *n'tomo* is a society of the young uncircumcised boys (*bila-koro*) in which they are instructed about the practices of communal life. They work together for their elders, organize a few festivities, practice a simple cult, and sometimes make sacrifices of lizards. The *n'tomo* mask, which belongs to the society, is danced either by an adult or by the children.

The *komo* is by far the most widespread and important society. It is accessible to all men after circumcision but barred to the *bila-koro,* the *jeli,* the women, and uninitiated foreigners. Masters of such societies are often blacksmiths or *wolo-so.* It is believed, indeed, that the manipulation of the magical powers related to the practice of the *komo* are dangerous, and that these powers strike back at the children of whoever uses them against others. But blacksmiths maintain their reputation of being great magicians by accepting such risks, while *wolo-so,* who lack immediate dependents because of their matrilineal status, have nothing to lose. Young boys are initiated into the *komo* in the year of their circumcision. They first go through a symbolic death, and are then shown the tricks through which the *komo* frightens the village people. From then on they are also in position, if they wish, to enter into a cycle of magical initiation leading to higher ranks in the society. The main function of the *komo* is to exert social control over the village life. It interferes continuously to frighten, punish, sometimes to poison whoever is guilty of serious offenses. The *komo* has been strongly opposed to Islamization, and it has also been used against colonial administration.

In order to balance the power of the *komo* and of its caste or slave leaders, the *horõ* lead another society, the *nama,* with approximately the same functions and organization.

We have very little information—and that not very reliable—on the *kono* and the *kore.* The latter is a gathering of young adults, and is associated with buffoonery and joking, somehow related to the *Koteba* theater, but in an obscure fashion.

One of the oldest associations is apparently that of the hunters. The hunters recruit members without consideration of age, caste, or class. The hierarchy among the hunters is founded on accomplishment, and, among people of equal achievement, age is taken into consideration to indicate the leaders. The hunters have their own exclusive cults, their secret knowledge and magic. They also have their own dances, songs, and *jeli* (*sere*) playing special musical instruments. They join together in large associations, often covering several villages (Y. Cissé 1964).

All these associations are closely linked to village activities and politics: agricultural work and hunts are undertaken by some associations; entertainment is given by the *flã-tõ;* village policing is done by the secret societies, and a certain equilibrium between the various social categories—noble and caste (or slave), youth and elders—is guaranteed through them.

From an early age until death, the men are taken into successive associations with specific purposes and overt discipline. Through these associations they are educated and learn to recognize their distinctive status in relation to each other and their position in the group as members at different levels of a complex but comprehensive society.

Many functions specifically linked to the village social environment and economics, particularly those related to agricultural work, will not be carried into town, while others, such as entertainment, will still find a *raison d'être* in urban life. But beyond its basic purpose, the discipline and rules of the association provide a general framework adaptable to new functions. In addition, the feeling that there is no proper integration into the social environment except through belonging to a cohesive and functional group is certainly strengthened when the people face the problems of a new urban milieu.

Part 2

THE ASSOCIATIVE
PROCESS

CHAPTER THREE

The Associations
of the Colonial Period

RECRUITING CRITERIA

THE first records relating to modern associations are found
in the files of the Department of the Interior. They are
limited to associations created before Independence—that is,
to a period extending from about 1940 to 1960. They form,
however, a useful introduction to our subject, covering a period
prior to our own investigation, on a broader, if shallower, basis
than direct observation allows. Considering them helps, therefore, to situate the associations both in time and in a more
general social and political pattern.

The official files of registered associations give the following
information: date of constitution, statutes and rules, records of
the organizational meeting, and a list of the leaders (sometimes
with their occupation). Not all the records are complete. The
law required notification of changes of the statutes, the pro-
ceedings, and, at each election, the names of the new officials,
but these last pieces of information are nearly always missing.
There is no information relating to the rank and file, not even
figures. From the available data, we have, as far as possible,
analyzed the purposes, recruiting, and functioning of the associations, and the social composition of the leadership.

Of course, the records cover only the associations with suf-
ficent organization to be able to go through the administrative

process of registration. Notwithstanding mergers of several of them (mostly political and athletic), there were 149 registered associations of African people during the forties and fifties. Most were registered between 1956 and 1959, with a peak in

TABLE 9

REGISTERED ASSOCIATIONS IN BAMAKO, 1930–60

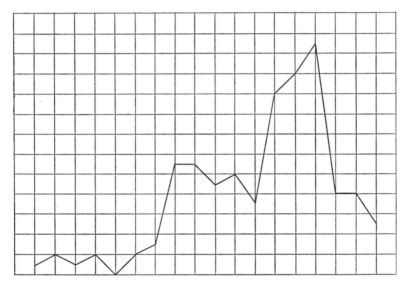

1930-1941-1946 1947 1948 1949 1950 1951 1952 1953 1954 1955 1956 1957 1958 1959 1960 After
  40   45

1958 (Table 9). This period coincides with the years of greatest political activity before Independence. Whatever their avowed purposes, all the associations were organized in an environment in which they could not avoid participating more or less directly in the political struggle (Table 10).

One can distinguish, by analysis of the titles and of the statutes, two kinds of associations: the first kind appeals to definite groups of people—youth, inhabitants from a particular

TABLE 10

YEAR OF ORGANIZATION OF DIFFERENT TYPES OF ASSOCIATIONS IN BAMAKO

(From the files of the *Direction de l'Interieur*)

	1930–40	1941–45	1946	1947	1948	1949	1950	1951	1952	1953	1954	1955	1956	1957	1958	1959	1960	1961	date not known	Total
Miscellaneous																1	1		1	3
Mutual Aid				1									1	1	4				1	8
Sport (private)			1			1	1	4	4	2	2	3	3	5	4	2		2		34
Sport (official)															1		6	3		10
Political				1				1		1			2	2	2	2	1		1	13
Cultural						1		1	1	1	1	1	4	3	1	1			2	17
Youth	1	1						2	2	2	2									10
Regional		1					1	2	1	2	3		7	7	6					30
Religious								1	1	1	2		1	1	5	2			2	16
Veterans and Alumni							1		2			3		1						7
Caste																			1	1
Total	1	2	1	2	0	2	3	11	11	9	10	7	18	20	23	8	8	5	8	149

TABLE 11

SOCIO-CULTURAL CHARACTERISTICS OF BAMAKO ASSOCIATIONS, 1930–60

PRIMARY CHARACTERISTICS \ SECONDARY CHARACTERISTICS	Mutual Aid	Sport (private)	Sport (official)	Political	Cultural	Youth	Regional	Moslem	Catholic	Veterans and Alumni	Ward	Occupation	Mixed	Army	Education	Caste
Mutual Aid											** ***	*	**			
Sport (private)	*					*		* * x		**	**** **** x	*** xxxx	*x			
Sport (official)							x								*x	
Political						*** xx		*					*			*
Cultural											*** **		*** **			
Youth																
Regional	***** ***** ***** xx		xx			xx						*x				
Religious (Moslem)	*** xxx															
Religious (Catholic)	***											xxx x				
Veterans and Alumni														** xx	*	
Caste	*														** x*	

x = another characteristic is noted in another box   * = single secondary characteristics area, members of religious persuasions, casted people, or veterans; the second kind emphasizes purposes independent of the recruiting criteria—mutual aid, sports, politics, cultural activities.

Recruitment and aims are, of course, often related. In order to discover any such correlations, we classified these associations by selecting as primary characteristics the driving purpose, or the criterion of recruitment stated in the title of the association, or the most obvious emphasis according to the by-laws, or the most strongly emphasized purpose during the history of the association, as is the case with political ones, whose real aims are not stated. We chose as secondary characteristics the subsidiary aims of recruiting criteria. On the basis, we worked out Table 11, which gives an idea of the most frequent combinations of the various socio-cultural characteristics. We can see, for instance, that regional associations nearly always state mutual aid as one of their aims; that political associations are usually related to the youth; and that athletic associations are often connected with the place of work. Conversely, we note that ward recruitment is favored by youth associations, and that mixed European-African societies usually follow sport or cultural pursuits.

Regional Associations

Of 149 registered associations, 30 were recruited on the basis of out-of-town origin. Instead of merely tribal or ethnic associations, we must speak of regional ones: twelve associations are declared to be open to natives of a definite city or town; eight to inhabitants from a *cercle;* three to those from a canton. We know already that tribes live intermingled in many rural areas and still more so in the cities. A geographical criterion of recruitment is not tribally segregative.[1] We found only two associations bearing a tribal name: one was created for political purposes but was never actually active (it was directed toward the *Malinke et Khassonke*); the other is

---

[1] An examination of the names and surnames of the officials of the regional associations always shows the mixing of various tribes.

Moorish but essentially open to all cattle breeders and strictly concerned with trade. Four associations were created by foreign migrants: two from Sénégal, one from Ivory Coast, and one from Upper Volta. A comparison with a map of the places of origin of Bamako inhabitants shows that most migrants were represented in town through one association (except the Guineans, whose associations apparently were not registered).

Regional associations are nearly always concerned with solidarity, sometimes vaguely formulated in the bylaws. An example is the association called *Originaires du Canton de Djitoumou,* created in 1955 "in consideration of the present difficulties of life and of the need of mutual acknowledgement and recriprocal help between the children of a same land [and because] many of our kinsmen, coming to Bamako meet enormous difficulties with food and board. . . ." The bylaws note also that students and workers were the promoters of the association and that old men and "notables" were ready to support it. No fees are called for; no specific forms of aid are defined.

In many other cases the bylaws provide for financial help and mutual assistance on occasions of baptism, circumcision, marriage, illness, death, and sometimes merely "misfortune." For instance, we find that the Wasulu Natives Association, from November, 1955, to February, 1957, spent 49,355 francs on the following occasions: twenty baptisms, six circumcisions, five marriages, ten deaths, one automobile accident, one disease, one robbery of garments, one jailing. The society numbered fifty-seven members when created. The fees amounted to fifty francs monthly until 1955 and one hundred francs thereafter. Special contributions for help were expected to run between five hundred and one thousand francs. The officers in 1955 included four clerks, one chauffeur, one potato seller, one health servant, and one shoemaker. In 1957 a woman was elected to the vice-presidency and another was chosen as a member of the board.

Since marriage is, in Bamana country and among related people, one of the main celebrations and an important social event, the regional associations nearly always organize an appropriate entertainment. It is sometimes specified in the by-laws that if the marrying member is a man he will pay for the celebration, but that a collection will be made in his favor; if it is a woman the association may cover the expenses.

Regional associations seldom declare any purpose except mutual help and entertainment. Two of them state that they have political educational purposes; two engage in sporting activities; two recruit among young people; and two are organized on an occupational basis. Monthly fees are rather low and vary from twenty-five to one hundred francs. Entrance fees are from two to five times the amount of the monthly fees. As mentioned above, special collections are made when a social event takes place.

Of a total of 245 people recorded among the officials of the 30 associations, employees of the government and of state enterprises are a majority (127); next come clerks (50); traders (37); craftsmen—modern (13) and traditional (7); and teachers (11). Others are not very numerous: five marabouts, two farmers, three "notables," two soldiers, and only one laborer and one professional. No women are recorded as officers, except the two mentioned above.

Obviously, the social composition of the officials is the result of a selective process and does not reflect the over-all composition of the association.

Religious Associations

Twelve religious associations are Moslem, and four are Catholic. Among the former, five were formed between 1954 and 1961 for the purpose of sending their members to Mecca. Four of them recruit on an occupational basis: policemen, railroadmen, health servants, and postmen. In all five, the members give a monthly contribution throughout the year, and each is elected in turn to collect the total amount to pay for a pilgrimage to the Holy Ground. The largest association counted sixty-three members and recruited without selective limitations.

The most important Moslem association was created in 1950 and revamped in 1954. It gathered all the *imam* [2] from Bamako, plus thirty-six marabouts and thirty-six eminent Moslems. Its aim was to teach the Koran, to build mosques, and to organize pilgrimages. In 1954 a female section was created, with seventeen women on the records.

As early as 1953, some believers worried about the existence of antagonistic sects and created an association to promote a better understanding among them. But in spite of this ecumenicity a Malchite association was founded in 1957. It was also a mutual aid association, helping members in case of baptism, marriages, circumcision, diseases, and arrests. Simultaneously, as we have mentioned above, the Wahabites drew together to promote modern Arabic schools.[3] Other Moslem associations promoted moral reformation, lowering of the dowry, or tried to teach modesty to college girls.

As is to be expected, the most numerous leaders have been marabouts and notables. Women also are numerous, since they are among the most devout Moslems.

The Catholic associations, usually created by priests or nuns, always number several clerics among their officers. Most of the associations have been formed for charity purposes. One was created in the Moslem model to send people on Christian pilgrimages.

Youth Associations

Of the ten youth associations recorded, four are Catholic. The other six state as their main purpose "to enhance weddings with songs and dances" or "to entertain the ward people." Some of them are typical dance societies, such as the *gũbe* or the *bara*. They carry European names: *Jeunesse Dorée de Dravéla; Jeunesse Florissante de Dar-Salam; Jeunesse-Club d'Hamdallaye*. As can be seen from the titles, the ward is the

---

[2] *Imam* is an Arabian word which means the leader of the prayer in the Moslem religion. Here it is the title given to the head of the mosque.

[3] Troubles occurred in Bamako in relation to these religious conflicts. *Medersa* were set afire and Wahabites were stoned in the late fifties (Chailley 1962).

basis for recruitment. There is no provision limiting admission to any social group, though it is understood that applicants must be young and preferably from the ward. Both sexes are admitted, but girls usually pay a lower fee than boys. The majority of the officials are clerks from private businesses (fifteen of forty-seven), employees from the government and state enterprises (thirteen), modern craftsmen, and traders.

PURPOSES

Political Associations

Because of the colonial situation, only six associations had an avowed political purpose, but at least thirteen could be considered to be directly linked to political action. Eight were created after 1956. Of the thirteen, five were associated with youth, two with education, one with religion, and one with an area.

The most active one, *Jeune Soudan,* was created in Paris by university students as early as 1951. The same year it joined a larger confederation, *Le Conseil de la Jeunesse,* also a front for political action. But this move opened a conflict inside the *Conseil* between R.D.A. and P.S.P. members. The latter were expelled and founded their own youth association. The same situation was repeated in 1957 when the two rival societies decided to merge, again to the benefit of the R.D.A.

Besides this militant association, there was also a chapter of the *Mouvement de la Paix* founded in Bamako in 1956, and an association promoting solidarity between people in Asia and Africa to fight colonialism founded in 1958. As a counter-move, the French administration tried to gain support from the Moslems, but in 1959 R.D.A. leaders established an Islamic cultural society with the declared purpose of modernizing education. The opponents to the R.D.A. helped to found an association of the traditional chiefs in 1956, as a section of a larger confederation covering former French West Africa.

Literate people, students, government employees, and traders were commonly the officers of these associations. According to the lists found in the records, we have the following figures for a total of 186 officers: civil servants, fifty; employees from state enterprises, twelve; merchants, thirty-nine; teachers, twenty; independent workers and craftsmen, nineteen; clerks from the private sector, eighteen; professional, eight; workers, seven; soldiers, six; chiefs, four; marabouts, three. We find also six priests and nuns, and five Europeans. There are a total of fifteen women. Among the names found on the lists, one can note many present government officials. Europeans and priests are listed invariably among the most conservative political associations.[4]

Sport Associations

The large number of sport associations (thirty-four private, plus ten official) is due both to the attraction of sport for Bamako youth and to the great variety of sport activities. Several of these associations were launched by the Catholic church as a means of attracting young men. But most of them recruited among people of similar occupation, or those working in the same enterprises. Occupation is stated in the titles of seven of them, and even when it is not mentioned in the name, examination of membership shows that many people of any single association belong to the same enterprise. Only two recruited membership on the basis of the ward, and one specified mutual aid as a secondary purpose. Leadership came almost exclusively from among wage earners in the public and private sectors. There were no independent workers and hardly any traders or businessmen, except in one association where they seemed to concentrate. Fees were usually not mentioned in the bylaws.

Today the government has reorganized and centralized sporting activities. Merging and federation of all the associations has taken place under the authority of the *Haut Commissariat à la Jeunesse et au Sport.*

---

[4] Several Frenchmen played important roles in the fight for Malian independence, but in a clandestine fashion.

Cultural Associations

The first cultural associations were created under the auspices of Europeans, usually teachers from the colleges. Soon the formula became popular among the African youth, especially those with education. The listing of the officials gives the following composition: again the public servants are most numerous (45 out of 103), next come the teachers (18), the clerks (16), the professionals (9), and the workers (6). There are very few craftsmen and merchants (five and three). As is to be expected, it is in these associations that we find the largest number of Europeans (twenty-six). Many are teachers, more often women than men. One association is obviously comprised of people of caste. None of them is linked to ward or enterprise recruitment.

The main activity of the cultural associations has been the theatrical performances of plays written by members, as theater is an old tradition among the Bamana. These plays were encouraged by French officials, and the African intelligentsia found them a potent means of political education and debate.

Today, cultural activities are concentrated in the official organization of the *Pionniers* for the children and the *Centres culturels*. Both will be described briefly in the next section.

Mutual Aid

Only eight associations list mutual aid as their primary purpose. Four of them recruit on the basis of the ward, one on occupational grounds (postmen), and one for pensioners and widows. Members are, for the most part, petty government employees, clerks from private business, wage earners, and a few modern craftsmen. There are no businessmen, merchants, or entrepreneurs. The membership of each association is probably not very large. The associations guarantee help in each usual event, but put some emphasis on illness and death. Entrance fees and monthly dues are not high, and it can be assumed that additional collections are made among the members.

It seems likely that this type of society is informal and unregistered, and that their actual number is higher than registration figures show.

The Labor Unions

Besides voluntary associations, the labor unions have played an important role in the political life of the city, and a few words should be said about them.

The first union that we found in the records was the *Syndicat des commis et interprètes* created in 1938; it was followed in 1944 by a C.G.T. union (Confederation Générale du Travail, a French leftist trade union) for low-ranking public servants. In 1946 a C.G.T. Confederation was created and gathered several unions from the public administration, the public enterprises such as the railroad, and the agriculturists. In 1947–48 there was a five-month strike—the second in the history of the railroad. In spite of violent repression, the workers won. It was one of the main events which caused the French to reconsider their colonial policy (O. Sembene 1960). In 1954 the same confederation organized a new strike, and the leaders were jailed. At this time *Force Ouvrière*, which had split off from the C.G.T. in France, tried to divide the Sudanese workers into a maze of competing craft unions. The files are stuffed with records of these hastily organized unions, which were, apparently, of short duration. The bulk of the workers remained with the C.G.T. until 1957, when they joined the African U.G.T.A.N. (*Union Générale des Travailleurs d'Afrique Noire*) led by Sekou Touré. At the same time a women's section was created.

CHAPTER FOUR

The Associations of the Post-Colonial Period

PRESENT-DAY ASSOCIATIONS

The Changing Pattern

IN the struggle against colonial rule, the associations were the stakes in the contests carried out among the political parties. Youth associations and regional associations were excellent fields of recruitment. The latter could be used, in addition, as a lever against the centralizing tendency of the U.S.–R.D.A. Attempts were made by the P.S.P. to lump together several regional associations from the eastern part of the country into a large political movement founded on tribal particularism and opposing the Songhai to the Bamana. To counter this threat, the U.S.–R.D.A. tried to unite, in a similar fashion, other tribal associations from the same eastern regions. In 1952, when this rivalry became dangerous for the colonial administration, both super-associations were dissolved. But a dangerous split had shown up, through these events, between the western and the eastern areas of the country, which are indeed loosely related on many accounts.

After Independence, there were serious troubles in the Ségou area. This unrest was led by a branch of one of the Ségou dynasties and had a definite regionalistic flavor. The new government felt compelled to repress the movement forcibly.

The suspicion of the new power toward associations in general, and regional ones in particular, was therefore aroused and legislation was passed in regard to "regionalism." The Constitution (Art. 4) states: "Any act of racial or ethnic discrimination, as well as any regionalistic propaganda carrying a threat against the security of the State or against the integrity of the territory of the Republic, is punishable by law." According to Article 55 of the Criminal Law (April 18, 1961), the penalty is from one to five years in jail, and eventually a five-to-ten-year prohibition from entering certain areas (*interdiction de séjour*), in case of such offenses. The law does not apply directly to the regional associations as such; they are tolerated, if registered as nonpolitical. But they may fall under its strict interpretation. Not knowing the exact terms of the law, people are only aware that regionalism is treated with suspicion and accordingly act with care. They often neglect to register their associations for fear of falling under some possible prohibition. In even the best instances they are content to make them known to the local *sous-section* of the party.

THE OFFICIAL ORGANIZATIONS

While the government tried to restrict the activities of associations founded on regionalism, the party attempted to mobilize the totality of the population into a large and comprehensive network of official organizations. The existence of these nonvoluntary associations delineates the field within which the voluntary ones will be able to exist, and they must be briefly described.

Since the victory of the U.S.–R.D.A., Mali is characterized by a single-party system. Every man and woman over eighteen must, in theory, join the party, buy a membership card, and attend the general assemblies. When this study took place, the city of Bamako was considered as a "section" of the national party and each city ward as a *sous-section*.[1] The *sous-section* is

---

[1] These classifications held true at the time of this study (1962). Organizational changes took place in Bamako in 1965–66.

divided into three committees: men, women, and young people, each with its own elected officials.[2] The men's committee leads the entire *sous-section*. They all meet together during the general assembly, once a month. The *sous-section* committee informs the *militants* of decisions made by the government or the party. It interests people in the life of the community. It organizes the *investissements humains* (collective work on utility projects), it deals with the ward schooling problems, with security in the streets for children, local hygiene, and the like. (It also collects money for governmental or party subscriptions.) Meetings of the *sous-section* are called *tō-sigi*, and the traditional procedure, such as the use of a *dalamina*, is still respected in some wards.

Besides the party, the labor unions are still the most important organizational structure. Thirty-two existing unions have been integrated into the official political life. One, the *Syndicat des Agriculteurs*, was dismantled in October, 1962, to prevent duplication and competition with the party and the official organization of the *Communes Rurales*. At the Congress of all the Malian unions in 1963, the unions were invited by the government to take a larger share in the management of the national economy and the state enterprises.

Youth associations and their memberships have been taken over by the national organization of the *Pionniers*. Membership in the *Pionniers* is compulsory for all young people of both sexes between the ages of eight and eighteen. The *Pionniers* are divided into three sets on the basis of age: the *minimes* (eight to twelve); the cadets (thirteen to fifteen); and the *pionniers* proper (sixteen to eighteen). From ages eighteen to twenty-five, members occupy responsible positions. In Bamako, each ward is the site of a local committee led by a "secretary of oriented activities," who is also a member of the ward's party Board. The Board of the *Pionniers'* committee is composed of seventeen boys and, since 1963, an equal number of girls. The

---

[2] This division has been altered since. Youth have now been incorporated into the adult committees.

local committee reports to the *Inspecteur de la Jeunesse* in Bamako, himself a subordinate of the *Commissaire aux activités dirigées,* who depends directly on the *Haut Commissaire à la Jeunesse et aux Sports.* The *Pionniers* organization has a double purpose: education and leisure. Children are taught citizenship, history, and a few notions about the working of the institutions. They are encouraged to collect folk songs, legends, and traditions. A competition is organized every year among all the committees: each must produce folk dances and skits of their own, preferably with a social meaning. The national winner is selected at a final competition.

Cultural activities are organized along somewhat the same lines. Cultural centers were created under French rule but reorganized by the new government and put under the authority of the *Haut Commissariat à la Jeunesse et aux Sport.* Such centers exist in practically every head-town. They recruit their leaders largely among young educated adults on a voluntary basis: teachers, doctors, veterinarians, midwives, nurses, and others. Every year, each center must prepare and present an original play, folk dances, and songs. Like the *Pionniers,* they enter into competition with the neighboring cities from the same *Région* and the best troupe from each *Région* is sent to Bamako in June for the final contest of the *Semaine National de la Jeunesse.* Each troupe performs before a select audience. A jury, made up of government and party officials, chooses the winner. Some of the dances and plays performed by these troupes are first-class shows.[3] The plays, though they always fall within the official party line, are bold attacks on ticklish problems, such as polygyny, forced marriage, caste prohibitions to marriage, abuses of Islam, or even criticism of the behavior of party officials (Hopkins 1964).

The weight of the official associations is considerable, and one can estimate that nearly a third of the active population are engaged in one or several of them.

[3] The National Troupe of Ballet, which is the culmination of this selective process, has won several international awards.

THE VOLUNTARY ASSOCIATIONS

It remains to be shown that all the corners of city life have not been integrated into the official structures. In spite of its inclination to control citizens' activities, the party tolerates a great many informal or even formal associations that exist outside it. Such associations are usually not registered. Therefore, they cannot be described in the same way as the colonial associations were. In any case, many of them have no names or bylaws to be analyzed.

Some associations are more popular and conspicuous than others. Some are restricted to closed circles and never appear in public; but others, such as the folk associations, perform on the streets, their performances being advertised by word of mouth among the members.

These performances are possible only in the dry season. The agricultural calendar from the villages is still one of the dominant criteria for making decisions about such activities—since the beginning of the dry season is the time for dances and celebrations in the bush, this rhythm of life is carried over into the city. A second calendar, a European one, is also superimposed in town. Government and school holidays and vacations take place in July and August, during the European summer and the middle of the rainy season in West Africa. Students, who are leaders in many activities among younger people, spend their time in European-inspired pursuits; at this time of year they give parties in the orderly framework of associations called "clubs."

In July of 1962, on our arrival in Bamako, we found these private entertainments in full swing, while folk associations were nearly dormant. Then, from October on, the clubs dwindled in importance and the folk associations took over until March or April. Certain associations, however, such as the mutual aid groups, have either permanent goals or target aims and are independent of climatic factors.

The large number of associations made it impossible to

investigate all. A complete survey was not feasible, although it would have been helpful to be able to situate each association within a general pattern. This is a statistical problem, and therefore not possible for a single field worker—although it would have been difficult, even with a team, to collect material such as lists of members and details of their origin and status, since inquiries on these matters are distrusted. For all the above reasons, a survey of such a wide field as Bamako, made by a single person, runs the risk of being superficial and unbalanced.

We were able to contact about twenty-five associations, not including the official ones. They can be roughly described as mutual aid, regional, youth, and entertainment associations. The sample covers several stages in a definite process of integration from rural to urban life and the transformation of the migrant peasant into a townsman. The associations attempt to fulfill two of the main requirements of modern industrial society: social security and social differentiation.

The prime need of the new city dweller, as sociologists have noted, is to set himself into a system of collective security comparable to that which was provided by the rural society—care of the sick and disabled, help in case of misfortune, and so on.

In Bamako, official social security was limited, until 1962, to public servants. Since then, it has been legally extended to all wage earners. The allowances cover marriage, birth, children's education, medical care, work casualties, and old age. Social security leaves out unemployment and death. Such a law is undoubtedly a great social achievement and liable to change the future conditions of rural migration. However, its application will be limited for a long time to the regular wage earners from public enterprises or modern business; it will overlook the apprentices and others working in the traditional sector and usually not registered as laborers, i.e., 36.5 per cent of the active male population in 1960, not including the seasonal workers. Furthermore, the present transitional economic situation is reducing the level of employment. A significant number of people will therefore be driven to seek security in spontaneous, popular associations.

These associations are not all limited to relief. There is no real security where there is no feeling of solidarity and belonging. Such feeling is gained through a close participation in family events, first among them being marriage. Weddings, not funerals, are the most important social events among the dominant populations living in Bamako. In the Bamana country, for instance, newlyweds are confined to their room for eight consecutive days, if the bride is a virgin, three days if she has been married before. During all this time, women of the families live on the premises to cook, sing, and dance. Kinsmen and friends of the couple come for visits and organize dancing once or twice a day. Musicians are hired; *griots* praise the couple and receive their share of gifts; cigarettes and refreshments are passed around. To organize these festivities and cover their costs, numerous *sociétés de mariage* are constituted. They are often impromptu, made up of friends of the couple. But practically no association, whatever its main purpose, fails to function as a *société de mariage* for its members. Entertainment, therefore, is one of the main activities of most mutual aid associations. It also becomes the driving purpose of some other associations, and eventually a means for people to get together on the basis of new social distinctions.

People do not come to town merely to reconstruct village institutions. Young men are trying to free themselves from patriarchal rule and sexual restraints. They seek ways to establish contacts in the city milieu. They come with expectations of a good job, better economic opportunities, and, more importantly, social advancement. Often, when they have fled from home, they must prove their social success in a tangible way. Associations may be a means of asserting their new freedom, of affirming their achievements in a milieu where social discrimination emerges from new and more highly rated standards. Social differentiation on the basis of modern Western standards goes with integration into the social milieu of the city. During this process, the criteria of recruitment change in the various associations that mark out this progress. Ethnic origin becomes less and less relevant as people assimilate themselves into the new pattern. Some of the young people born or raised in town tend to associate on the basis of neighborhood; others, at a higher level of integration, group together on the basis of social achievements. These are the three steps toward integration, and we shall observe this process as we study voluntary associations in Bamako classified according to their two main activities: mutual aid and entertainment.

Mutual Aid Associations

Settlement in town is not usually completed in a single move. It is, rather, a process.

The biographies we collected show a typical pattern of immigration: a young man goes to school in a small town near his village; at the end of his elementary studies, he finds no employment worthy of his literacy. The feeling of losing a precious investment is very keen, both for the young man and for his family. Someone, therefore, advises him to go to Bamako where opportunities are greater. After working at some manual or craft job for several months, the young man saves enough money to pay for the trip to town. His parents (usually the mother) may be reluctant; but sometimes he is blessed by his father. He has the addresses of a kinsman, a friend of the family, or a schoolmate's kinsman living in Bamako, whom he will contact upon his arrival. His host will feed him and give him a place to sleep in his compound; in return, the young migrant will work every Sunday for his benefactor. Both friends from his home village and his neighbors in Bamako will help him find a job. Successive periods of work and unemployment will follow, each lasting several months. Then some accident occurs: the father dies at home, or the migrant himself is injured or becomes sick. In other cases, when he has left home against his parents' will, he may be taken back by the police. He returns, therefore, to his family and will spend several months, sometimes several years in the village. After a while, the original problem of finding a rewarding job comes up again, and again the same expedients are used to find one's way to the capital. In a few instances, a migrant may return to his village three times or more before settling permanently in the city.

Variations to this pattern are also found for illiterate young men. Instead of coming directly to Bamako, they may try to earn money, either abroad, in Ivory Coast, or in such enterprises as gold mining in the Boure country (on the Guinean border). After more or less fortunate experiences they will try Bamako, either as a crown of their success or as a last expedient.

The first generation of migrants almost never marries in town. They are often already engaged to girls at home, or they return to their villages after a few years to find wives. Indeed, most consider that city girls are too whimsical, lavish, and lazy. On the other hand, they praise the submissiveness, fidelity, and working capacity of country girls.

In summary, ties with the home town are very close for first-generation migrants, at least during the early years. The associative process is clearly related to this fact.

In the following examples, we shall see how the support for mutual help and social security shifts from informal groupings of rural origin to more precisely urban structures.

A compound in town will serve as the rallying point for people from a given village or a given area. It is usually the dwelling of an elder long settled in the city. A few scattered blocks are known as being populated by Moorish, Songhai, Hausa, or as the meeting place of people from some provincial town. The Miñāka colony still maintains a brightly colored hut in Dar-Salam, close to a sacred tree where they sacrifice dogs every year. But neither housing facilities nor administrative policy permits such clustering to become of significant importance. Most people from a common stock, therefore, live apart, and they are satisfied to have a permanent meeting place at someone's house. It is common to find among such groups a man of caste who knows everyone and where they live. Soon he becomes the necessary intermediary between all of them, and he encourages solidarity among people of the same village or the same town. By these activities, which are part of the traditional tasks of the *ñamakala*, he becomes the active collusive agent of an otherwise loose sort of association.

This is the case of the association of people from Mourdiah, a town of 2,000 inhabitants in the Sahel 190 kilometers north of Bamako. The main families of Mourdiah are the Diara (Bamana), the Kamara (Soníke), the Traoré (Fula), and the Makãgile (Moors of Tichit assimilated by the Soníke). Each is represented in Bamako. Some are cattle traders, others are public servants, male nurses, mattress makers, and so on. They live in widely separated wards: Bagadadji, Médina-Coura, Dar-Salam, and Hamdallaye. *Jeli* and *june* people often come from Mourdiah during the dry season to practice a trade or simply to put themselves in the service of a wealthy urban family. Some of them stay permanently. As one of their chores they serve as messengers among the urban dwellers from their home town. They keep the older men informed of news from home and from everyone else in town. Together with them, the elders discuss problems of general interest to people of Mourdiah settled in town and make decisions accordingly. For instance, when a mosque was built in Mourdiah, the *ñamakala* made a collection among the natives of the area living in Bamako. They made another collection when it was decided to send Malian flags home. Recently, an old man who wished to return home gave notice to the elders, who instructed the *ñamakala* to collect money for his trip.

Such an "association" is very loose and in a sense hardly deserves the title. There are no fees, no periodic meetings, no appointed leaders. It operates on the assumption that the people from Mourdiah who dwell in Bamako are still citizens of their home town. It is the prolongation into the city of village life and loyalties; it carries into town the concerns and problems of the village. However, there are probably as many of these groupings in Bamako as there are towns represented. They cover the entire city with an invisible network, reaching people at all social levels. To try to avoid such "associations" is considered a mark of egotism, a rejection of the old customs and values, tantamount to breaking relationships with home. The leaders of these groups and the *ñamakala* are the most eager to maintain such contacts and types of security through the "association." They impose it upon the younger generations who accept it, sometimes with reluctance. But few people in Bamako are in a position to break away from the rural world.

Foreigners, or people from far-away and culturally different areas, organize themselves for mutual help on a national or ethnic basis. But since they come from more distant and larger areas, they recruit among people who do not necessarily know each other, even indirectly, and here formal organization replaces personal ties.

Such associations, closely linked to the place of origin, are restricted to a certain kind of assistance related to "home." The main fear of migrants whose families are in the bush is that they may die away from their kinsmen. A young man fears that after returning home to marry a country girl, he will have to leave her with his family for several years before she can join him in town. Thus, home remains a dominant concern, and as long as it stands as a possible retreat, one must maintain one's rights as a villager.

As for settled migrants, the problem is no longer to return home before dying but to insure security for one's family in town. Fellow villagers are not necessarily the best fitted to help in such instances. They will turn rather toward people who are in a similar position, people who are settled in town with a job and a regular income, i.e., fellow workers. Associations founded among wage earners in the same enterprise—public offices or private businesses—are commonly interested in death insurance. In the *Mutuelle des P.T.T.* (Postmen), for instance, members pay a monthly fee of one hundred francs so that in case of death their widows will receive an allowance of fifty thousand francs, plus ten thousand francs for each child. The *Mutuelle* does not cover any other risk, nor does it carry out any kind of celebration.

Although a great many young men return home to seek

wives, more and more of them marry in town. According to the census data (*Etudes Demographiques* 1960), in nearly half of the households one spouse was born in Bamako, and in 12 per cent both of them. Marrying is a different problem for the young men born in town than it is among the peasantry, though some of its features have been maintained. Freer choice of a partner is easier in the city. But the suitor must find some way to compensate for the moral guarantee that a large and well-known lineage would represent in the village. He must try to impress his girl's family favorably even though he may have no relatives in town. When he is engaged, the custom is that he visits his future affines and offers kola nuts. Of course, he is no longer requested to work for the father of the bride, as he would be in the country, but he is appreciated all the more if he comes accompanied by as many *terike* (friends) as possible—a man with friends is a man to be trusted. When he is to be married, the young man needs money to pay for the celebration and friends to attend the ceremony and visit him and his bride during the eight days of customary retirement. Many regional associations fulfill such purposes. Through them, the groom can find an elder to recommend him to his fiancée's family, and will be able to bring an impressive escort to the ceremony.

This is also the purpose of some nonregional associations for the young people born in Bamako. *Société d'Aide et de Coopération* (S.A.C.) is the present title of an association created in 1960 by a group of young men who were childhood friends and lived in two neighboring wards, Bagadadji and Niaréla. Originally, they numbered about fifteen: tailors, chauffeurs, commissionaires, public servants, and the like. The society was created to assist its members in various social events, and the original idea was to give two thousand francs for a marriage and one thousand francs for a baptism. The monthly fees were set at two hundred francs. During the first month, the association met about three times, but it did not contribute to any event. At this time an attempt was made to increase the membership, and the members contacted more childhood friends, former school fellows, or neighborhood acquaintances. This campaign seems to have been successful, for the membership more than doubled. Among the new recruits, five had a better education, and they suggested the writing down of the bylaws, the formation of a board, and the registration of the association. They also gave the society its present name. The entrance fees were set at between five hundred and five thousand francs and were computed according to the marital situation of the recruit: a bachelor not engaged to be married would pay the minimum—five hundred francs; if engaged, he would pay according to the expected date of his wedding—if the marriage were to take place within a month, he paid the maximum fee. In return, the association was to pay two thousand francs for a baptism and seventy-five hundred francs for first and second weddings. Although some members suggested that the association pay only five thousand francs for the second wedding, and twenty-five hundred for any subsequent one, this proposition was rejected. The bylaws do not provide for contributions for circumcisions, funerals, illnesses, or unemployment. However, if members are ill or unemployed, they are exempted from paying the monthly fee. To provide the association with income, public balls are organized. The association hires an orchestra, rents a ballroom, and advertises. Four balls were organized between 1960 and 1963. The association meets three Sundays a month. Absence and delays without excuses are fined twenty-five to fifty francs. Every year the members celebrate together the anniversary of the association with a private dance.

In February, 1963, the association numbered forty-one members, all between twenty and thirty years old. All were born in Bamako or had come to town at an early age. Twenty were married. Neither tribal origin nor caste is relevant except to show that there is no discrimination on this ground: sixteen are Bamana or Manïka, five Moorish, three Fula, three Sonïke, two Kagoro, and nine people are of caste. Professionally, we find ten public servants, eight clerks, seven tailors, three repairmen, two photographers, five traders, two carpenters, two peddlers, and one chauffeur (plus three in unspecified jobs).

More than half of the members are illiterate. The board has twelve members, five coming from the original association. The president is a tailor, single and illiterate. He initiated the founding of the association and has been president since the beginning. This was the main reason given for his re-election. Although he is not the eldest member, he was appreciated as a man to be trusted and one who never has had trouble with his companions. The vice-president, our informant, is a tabulator-equipment operator, literate and more recently recruited. He is entrusted with all the papers of the association.

The other positions on the elected board are: *secrétaire general, trésorier, commissaire aux comptes, conseillers techniques, organisateur, commissaire à la propagande,* and *secrétaire adjoint.* Three people of caste are members of the board. A smaller body of six people, the *Conseil de discipline,* meets more often. Its purposes are not what its name would suggest; the *Conseil* is not empowered to judge conflicts arising between members. Though it does consider any cases of expulsion, usually for nonpayment of the dues, it is primarily an execuive body. It is also in charge of computing the entrance fees. The board is re-elected every four months by the general assembly. It submits to the latter the names of the candidates for the *Conseil de discipline.*

Of the original recruits, six have left—three have gone abroad on duty, one is in jail, and two were expelled for nonpayment of the dues. Between 1960 and 1963, the association celebrated eighteen marriages and seven baptisms.

When a member becomes engaged, the rules do not prescribe that the other members go with the groom to visit the in-laws. Such groups of friends are impromptu and are constituted independently. Of course, belonging to the association is a great help in this matter, but to restrict the group to friends from the association would exclude other friends. Friendship and affinity are not confounded with the joining of an association marked by a definite socio-economic purpose. However, the association does send delegates on the wedding day to pay the allowance publicly and introduce its members to the kinsmen of the newlywed. During the following week, all members must visit the couple at least three times.

The social activities of the association go beyond the strict application of the rules. In the beginning, members met informally under a shelter built outside the vice-president's compound, to talk or to play association-owned games. It was their *grē*. Unfortunately, the shelter caught fire, and since then the *grē* has been dissolved. On a friendly basis again, but not according to the statute, the association would give a farewell party to a good and devoted member when, for instance, he was appointed abroad.[4] This was the case for the former vice-president, a chauffeur sent to the Malian Embassy in the United States. All his friends from the S.A.C. met at his home for a dance, and refreshments were paid for out of the association's funds. Activities of this kind are very like those of the clubs, which we shall investigate later. Though it is not impossible that the S.A.C. may turn itself into a club, its chief and nearly exclusive purpose when it was founded was related to the formation of a family and not the organization of entertainment.

It is a common aspiration among young townsmen to gain some freedom and initiative in marital matters, and, it is therefore not surprising to learn that there are several associations of this particular kind in Bamako. Many young friends from a single ward organize themselves on similar bases. The ward, indeed, is usually the first recruiting ground for young people who were born in town and who met each other either in school or in the streets. It is also an easy definition of the limits of the association and an inducement for other ward dwellers to join. The ward is also the resuscitation of the territorial village unit catering to the more or less obscure wish to organize people along the lines of the former, well-coordinated society.

Unfortunately, however, ward limits do not enclose a similar ordered reality as in the old village, and this standard of recruitment must give way to new considerations. In Dar-

---

[4] The creation of a diplomatic corps in 1960 has been the occasion of numerous appointments abroad.

Salam, for instance, an association similar to the one described above does exist as the *Association d'Entr'aide de Dar-Salam*. To the territorial criterion of recruitment is added the further restriction of the entrance fee of 5,000 francs and monthly dues of 250 francs. Thus the social situation—wealth—has become the dominant factor of recruitment, and since this ward, which is one of the oldest, has been deserted by the wealthiest people, membership dropped from thirty-two members in 1959 to sixteen in 1962.

The S.A.C., on the other hand, though it recruits mostly among people from two neighboring wards, has not set territorial limitations on its membership. It represents, from this point of view, a more adaptive type of association.

Weddings and baptisms are also the concern of city women. At the time of a wedding, women from both families, as well as acquaintances, visit the bride, offer her garments, and stay the full week of the celebration to prepare the food, wash the clothes, and entertain each other. At the end of the seclusion period of the newlyweds, they help the bride cook her first conjugal meal.

At a baptism, while the men have met early in the morning to name the baby, women meet in the afternoon at the mother's kinsmen's place to offer scarves and loincloths.

In the bush, women used to spin the thread for the cloth they intended to offer or bought gifts from money they earned through the sales of produce on the market. In the city such activities are often not permitted, and opportunities to earn money are few. Women must depend more on the generosity of their husbands or kinsmen to obtain money for their gifts. The formation of mutual aid societies is, therefore, a way for women to maintain a degree of freedom.

Such a women's association was created in Bagadadji in 1959. At that time, all men and women were already organized within the U.S.–R.D.A. party, as explained before, and were divided among elders and younger people. When President L.S. Senghor from Sénégal came for an official visit to the country, each ward was invited to participate in the official parade. The

Bamako. Inside the *du-kene*

Building in the African ward

The koranic
school

A sheep herder

Above left: Laundrymen

Above right: Cobbler (*garāke*)

Below: Hairdresser and President
of the Dunūba

The Imam

Blackening the gums

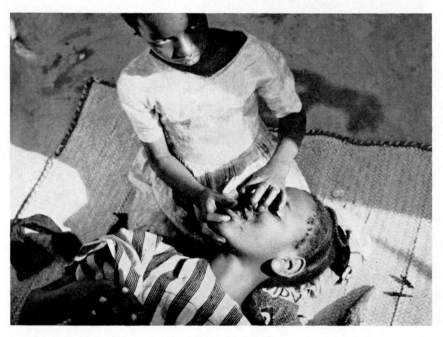

Upper left: Regional troupe
of Timbuctu

Upper right: Regional troupe
of Mopti

Below: Women's militia at the
Independence celebration

Association
des Chasseurs du Mali

The *gūbe* drums

Hunter's *semi*

Segu-ka-bara drums: the *cu*, the *gelegele-bani*, the *gãgã*

Jarawara dancers

Kono mask

young men of Bagadadji suggested for the first time that their wives take part in this reception. The following day, one of the young women, N.T., suggested to two of her friends, R.C. and F.K., that they create a *tõ* of the younger women of the ward to prepare for this celebration and to continue as a mutual-aid society. Together they approached an older woman, M.S., who knew a great many ward dwellers, and she approved the idea. They instructed a *jeli-muso*, B.K., to tell other *muso-mise* (young women) in Bagadadji that a *muso-mise-tõ* was being created and that the organizational meeting would take place on the following Sunday. About fifty women were present at the organizational meeting. Most of them already knew each other, either because they had played together as children or because they had met at weddings. The purpose of the proposed association was explained by N.T., the initiator of the idea, to be enlistment of women to participate in parades and to aid at weddings, baptisms, or circumcisions within the members' families.[5] The weekly fees were set at twenty-five francs and the allowance for celebrations at two thousand francs. Meetings were to take place every Sunday. A board was elected: M.S., a *fula-muso*, was appointed *Présidente*, because she was the oldest and also because she was very popular among the women of the ward. The next in age—another Fula woman—was elected *vice-présidente*, while R.C., and her friend F.K., both Bamana, were appointed *trésorières* in consideration of their education. N.T., the protagonist, a former school girl, younger than the other women, was elected *secrétaire* in charge of keeping the records of the association. Another Toucouleur woman was given the title of *secrétaire à l'organisation*, while B.K., the *griote*, was officially designated as the *tõ-jeli*.

To join the *tõ*, women had to be married, widowed, or divorced, but they could not be *muso-koroba* or elder women, i.e., mothers of married women with children, since the latter already had their own *tõ* within the party. Other than these age

---

[5] The degree of kinship was limited to first cousins on both sides.

limitations, there were no official restrictions. Indeed, women of several ethnic groups or castes did join, even foreign women. Actually, nearly all of the members were born in Bamako; in spite of the fact that only three were literate and few could speak French, they all were wives of well-to-do people—civil servants, merchants, small businessmen, and members of the U.S.–R.D.A. None were the wives of migrant dwellers, or of people of inferior status.

The *muso-mise-tõ*, though not an official section of the party, was invited to send two representatives to the ward party committee. The main activities of the women were attendance at weddings in which some of the members were taking part and participation in official parades. In view of this last purpose, they each bought a uniformed *taille-basse* [6] of the same fabric. After the first Independence Day Celebration in 1960—in which they participated in their uniforms—many women left the ward, and the *tõ* disappeared.[7]

Entertainment and Folk Dance Associations

In the associations discussed above, emphasis was on mutual aid. Although some associations are restricted to that purpose, others have entertainment activities on the side.

Mutual aid and entertainment are certainly not exclusive,

---

[6] This unusual French expression means literally "low waist." It designates a tight blouse, which is in fact not low, without sleeves and with gathered flounces around the waist.

[7] The tontine or *esusu* (Bascom 1952) system has been described many times. It exists in Bamako under the name of *pari*. (*Pari* means, in French, "bet." As is often the case, the French word has deviated from its original meaning. On the other hand, the word *tontine,* which is used by Frenchmen to describe the system, is used in Bamako to translate the phonetically closer Bamana word *tõ*. The linguistic confusion is completed by the fact that the original Neapolitan meaning of *tontine* designates an old institution noticeably different from what it describes today.) Every participant contributes a fixed amount of money periodically to the common fund, and each one in his turn receives the entire amount collected.

Today this institution is formed primarily in order to save money for pilgrimages to Mecca. It is usually organized among people working in the same enterprise. However, it is apparently far more common among women, either from the same neighborhood or from the same mosque, and usually has a more mundane purpose.

but we find that, at a certain point, one purpose is often stressed at the expense of the other. When social security—which is more than mutual aid—is involved, it stands as the main goal and basis for organization. As we shall see, when an entertainment association lends support for mutual aid, it never goes much beyond the program of a marriage society. When social definition or promotion is the primary purpose, then entertainment becomes the leading feature of the association and the foundation of its organizational structure.

In the following pages we shall describe entertainment associations and their capacity to integrate their members into the social life of the urban milieu. Though several types of these associations exist concurrently, they actually illustrate a process. Age of the members, social criteria of recruitment, relationship between sexes, internal organization, as well as musical and dancing features, change in a comprehensive fashion in a process of social escalation, emerging from the rural world and aiming at near identification with Western standards.

Entertainments in Bamako

When asked why they like the city, many people mention the movies as one of the main attractions, though they may attend rarely. There are eight movie theaters in town: three are located in the central commercial section; the others are in the African wards. Seats cost from fifty francs to two hundred francs. The attraction of the movies is so strong, especially for the youth, that some boys, after earning their daily fifty francs at the market carrying baskets for European ladies, attend every night. Seeing the same show several times in a row is not uncommon. Married men of the petty bourgeoisie go to the movies on Saturday night with boy and girl friends, but usually without their wives. The latter attend less often, and with other women from their wards. Girls sometimes ask their boy friends for movie money, as it is not yet common, except in the most Westernized society, for people of both sexes to go out together. There is always a crowd of young men at the doors of the movie houses, standing and chatting loudly during the

entire performance. It is a common meeting place. Cigarette
peddlers, soda sellers, women petty traders sit near the entrance, while a few prostitutes stand at the edge of the lighted
area.

Theater performances are given in the street by the *Koteba*
(Meillassoux 1964), and occasionally by the *Pionniers* ward
section in the school building or outdoors. Admission is charged
for *Pionniers'* shows, which are attended by the ward residents.
In June, during the *Semaine de la Jeunesse,* theatrical performances take place every night in the building belonging to the
party. During the same month, the various colleges in town
give their farewell performances. These are attended by people
from the upper social strata, often government ministers and
high officials of the party. On Sunday afternoons soccer
matches and horse races attract great crowds.

Balls have become a favorite entertainment for the emanci-
pated youth. Several ballrooms exist in town, and public buildings—such as the *Maison des Combattants, Maison des Pionniers,* or *Maison du Parti*—are occasionally rented for the
purpose. Local orchestras, belonging to the *Troupe Nationale,*
play Caribbean music or Congo-Leo "typicals." Balls usually
take place at the beginning of the rainy season when the
students are ready to leave school or on national or religious
holidays, sometimes for no other purpose than to collect money
for an organization. Most are sponsored by an official or private association. Admission fees are as high as three hundred
francs for a man; girls usually are admitted free.

People of modest means who do not attend such costly
entertainments are content with the *balani-dõ.*[8] One or two *bala*
musicians settle on one side of a dirt street accompanied by
jẽbe drummers.[9] People who wish to dance give twenty-five

[8] *Bala* (wooden xylophones). There are two kinds of *bala;* a large one,
which can be played by anyone, is said to be the *Sikasso-bala;* a smaller one is
restricted to the *jeli* of caste. *Balafo* (*fo,* to greet or to play an instrument),
Balani-dõ (*dõ,* to dance). The *balani-dõ* is usually played in the streets by non-
casted musicians on the *Sikasso-bala.*

[9] *Jẽbe* (variety of drum) ; see description below in relation to the *Sogonī-kũ,*
pp. 96–100.

francs to the players for each group of four dancers. Women, who are considered as *cõpani*,[10] do not pay.

At a more private level, and especially important for women, who usually do not attend the above entertainments, marriage celebrations are occasions for dancing. They get together to hire *griots* and musicians for a whole afternoon or evening of dancing.

When they are not attending these entertainments, women spend most of their leisure chatting within the ward. Men prefer not to stay home with the women, but join their friends at their *grẽ*. The *grẽ* is a meeting place where the men come to chat, discuss, or report on city gossip. They are sometimes called such names as *"L'O.N.U."* or *L'Assemblée Nationale* because political debates are among the favorite topics. A *grẽ* usually is a gathering of friends from various wards who happened to know each other at school or at work, and who are therefore people of similar social status. *Griots* are, nevertheless, always welcome in these groups, in which they either fulfill their usual functions (calling on the members, giving notice of the meeting or events interesting the group, or entertaining their friends) or belong as regular members. The *grẽ* meets permanently, but attendance is larger at night. These gatherings rarely exceed twenty people, and the entire group meets together only rarely. As a meeting place, the men choose the shop of one of their friends, often a tailor,[11] or any convenient spot where they bring benches and chairs, which are eventually sheltered under a thatched roof. Whenever a new member is introduced into the *grẽ*, it is customary to ask for a gift of money and kola nuts, which are shared among everyone. People from the same *grẽ* sometimes organize picnics or other collective amusements.

[10] From the French: *accompagnée*. Accompanied girls usually do not pay at ballrooms.

[11] Tailors are a social nexus in Bamako society. During the day girls like to sit and lounge around the shop in the proximity of the beautiful dresses and clothes. Some shops are known as the scene of gallant encounters. It is a standard joke to say that tailors take advantage of the demands of their work in petting their pretty customers while taking their measurements. Tailors are said also to be great gossips.

This brief survey of the entertainments offered by the city shows that, although they look numerous when listed, they are in fact few. Each is available only to a fraction of the people, according to sex, age, or social condition. Associations are still, therefore, a major source of enjoyment for their members and of entertainment, through folk dances, for the ward.

The Musicians

Folk dance associations are probably not as numerous in Bamako as are mutual aid societies, since it is necessary, in order to found a folk dance association, to recruit artists, musicians, and dancers.

As we know, the *griots* are musicians and artists by virtue of their caste membership, though every *griot* by birth is not compelled to become a musician. The *griots'* fields of artistry are clearly delineated: they have exclusive musical instruments, songs, and dances.

On the other hand, *griots* exist only among certain ethnic groups. They are most numerous and culturally integrated among the Manīka, the Sonīke, and the Fula. They are less numerous among the Bamana and the populations from the Niger Valley. They do not exist among people living in the south and southeast, forest tribes, or the Miñāka-Senufo group.

The *griots* cannot, therefore, claim a monopoly on music and dance, and in fact they do not. Any gifted man can play drums, *Sikasso-bala,* or stringed instruments, such as the *juru-kele* (single-string guitar) or the *soku* (violin). Hunter bards are not people of caste, and they play the *semi,* a stringed instrument similar to the *kora,* which is exclusively a *griot* instrument. Anybody with talent can sing or dance, within the limitations imposed by their sex and social rank. The *griots* were originally court musicians, and therefore are associated mostly with ceremonies; the other artists have no special status and participate in any kind of popular entertainment.

In the bush, they usually belong to one of the many young people's societies. They are selected solely on the basis of their talent and learn with the help of a skilled friend. They may belong to any social clan or caste, even *griot,* though in that case they do not perform as representatives of their caste. Actually, drummers are often blacksmiths, *wolo-so,* or, to a lesser extent, *horõ.* Musicians traditionally are not paid, but when there is a performance they may go among the crowd, greet some of the eminent people, and receive money.[12] Money is also given to congratulate the dancers, either spontaneously or because of a challenge: the dancer invites someone to come and do as well as himself; if the challenged person refuses, he acknowledges the superiority of the other by pouring bank notes on his head. All the money is shared equally among the dancers and the drummers. Drummers are supposed to be capable of building their instruments, stretching and replacing the heads. As a rule, the instruments do not belong to them, but to their association.

Jarawara

One well-known folk dance group in Bamako is *jarawara,* sometimes also called *Sogo,* which performs on occasional Saturday afternoons near Niaréla's market place. *Jarawara* (the lion) is the name of one of the several masks which are exhibited. *Sogo* (which means game or meat) designates them in a more general way.

A small band of a few *jẽbe* and a chorus of women stay inside the shadows of the market buildings; they play and sing loudly, inviting young men from the group to come before the drums and perform a few fast stomping steps. The crowd, consisting mostly of children, women, and young men of peasant origin, is kept away from the center of the area by a member of the association.

From the bush next to the market place where they are hidden, masks come out one after the other, led by a couple of young men, their heads covered with scarves until they reach

---

[12] In some areas, the local drummers make up a sort of musical "picture" of each man in the village. When they beat that rhythm on the occasion of a celebration, the man who identifies it as his must come forward, dance or talk, and give money to the drummers.

the dancing ground. Most of these masks are made of a bulky wooden frame covered with printed cloth, which is about the height of a man, a meter wide, and a meter and a half long. The huge body is topped by the head mask fixed on the end of a long flexible neck, entirely covered with the same fabric. At the sound of the drums, the bulky "animal," animated by two young men hidden below, starts wandering heavily around and moving its head up and down and sideways in rhythm. Many masks are representations of horned and bearded animals, ceaselessly moving the head in every direction. The *kono* (bird) has an articulated beak, and it imitates the sharp jerky movements of the animal's head, occasionally picking its body in search of parasites. A more recent figure wears on the back a couple of articulated puppets of a man and a woman, moving the arms up and down and twirling around. During the dance, the young men who led the mask from the bush continue to guide it around, preventing the fabrics from getting entangled in the feet of their comrades underneath.

A few of the masks are different. The lion, for instance, has a smaller and more realistic body, animated by a single dancer. It comes on all fours, crouches down on two false forepaws, waves its head, bounces on frightened hunters played by confederates from the group, and frightens the children a little. One mask is a feminine figure, today called *la princesse*. She usually stands still, moving only her arms and head in imitation of feminine attitudes.

The *jarawara* of Bamako is a *barañini* (seasonal workers) association. Its membership, which is mostly Bamana, comes from the Tchero area in the *Cercle du Macina*. The association is the transplantation into town of a *sāsani-tō* entertainment common in this area. The masks are said to be Bamana, although the puppets may have been borrowed from the Bozo.

Recently, the members have appointed the eldest, who may be around twenty-seven years old, as their leader. In contrast with the others, he is married and has become a permanent resident in Bamako. Through him, the group has put itself under the auspices of the Niaréla *sous-section* of the

U.S.–R.D.A. The party local has offered them the fabrics which are used to cover the bodies of the masks.

The group has little activity beyond the organization of the dances, and it can hardly be described as an association. Members do not pay any fees or dues; they have no regular meetings. It is neither a mutual aid nor a marriage society. In effect, membership is made up exclusively of healthy young workers with no other prospect in town than to work for six months at the most and then return home for the agricultural tasks of the rainy season.

The *Jarawara*'s performances, nevertheless, have become such a success, that after the group had been used by the *sous-section* to greet the President of Mali on his return from a trip abroad, their dances were included as a repeated feature in the official parades.

Therefore, as the traditional young men's *tõ*, it still contributes to the entertainment of the people of the "village" (here, the ward). It is no longer associated with the tasks of the community, but with the political fortune of the *sous-section*. It has even been promoted to the rank of official folklore.

If it were an association in the full sense of the term, *jarawara* could still not be considered as an efficient institution of social promotion and integration into urban life. The fame of the group is founded on its folkloric (i.e., village) origin, which the members cannot therefore reject. Stressing origin is the most immediate way to assert their personalities in the competitive urban milieu, but they do not learn through it new and adequate knowledge for urban adjustment. A carry-over from the village, *jarawara* makes the young villager welcome in town as an exotic peasant. This "association" is a projection of village ways into the urban milieu. It is an urban phenomenon only because it stands on the basis of a rural particularism, opposed to similar exotism imported from other villages.

Dunūba

Dunūba (large drum) is the name of a traditional warriors' dance, closely related to the age-set system of the Kouroussa area, on the upper Niger River, in the Manīka country of the Republic of Guinea.

In this area a group of several generations of circumcised young men between fifteen and twenty-five to twenty-eight years of age constitutes what is sometimes called a *tõ nioxo mõ* (those who are together in a *tõ*), the equivalent of the Bamana *flã-bolo*. These men of fighting age prove their strength and courage by dancing the *dunũba*, which is a dance of flagellants. The dancers tie a handkerchief as a bandeau around the head, wear either a *bila* wrapped around the waist and between the thighs or a *kurusi* (large baggy pants). On both arms magic leather bangles sustain their strength; in one hand they carry a small war ax or a saber, in the other a *wene* (short whip) made of the plaited membrane of a donkey's penis. They walk in single file around the *bara* (dance ground), each whipping the man in front of him until the blood runs. Those who cannot bear the pain leave the file amidst the jeers of the crowd. When only four or five of the fifteen young men are left, the remaining ones come in the middle of the ground to dance and be nursed by the women and to whip each other again until they are stopped by the crowd. After they retire to rest, women and young girls come in to dance and sing the praises of the brave ones. They are followed by the *tiekoroba* (old men) with a glorious past, but without the strength to whip themselves any longer. The *dunũba* formerly was danced only at great occasions, to celebrate a victory or a circumcision. Today, in the bush, the most usual occasion is at circumcision time.

In Bamako, the *dunũba* is danced by an association of Manīka young men founded in 1952 and renewed in 1958 when a full generation (about twenty men) left to be replaced by a new set of sixteen, according to the traditional pattern of age-set renewal. Recruitment is not, in theory, limited to people from Kouroussa, and anybody from Bamako can join. The *ñamakala* are accepted on an equal footing. But the *wolo-so*, cannot dance, because the *dunũba* rhythms are *horõ*. At present, all of the members (about twenty) were either born in

Kouroussa or born to people from that area. Except for the leader, they are not married. Most are illiterate, with little knowledge of French. They all have low-income jobs: bakery workers, cart drivers, laborers, and so on. Many of them are still seasonal workers. They live in various sections of the town, but their *grē* is at the edge of Bolibana, near the *petit marché de Ouolofobougou* at the barber stand kept by the group's president, a man of thirty, who was our main informant. He told us that he was elected because he was the eldest and was also considered serious and responsible.

The entrance fee is set at one hundred francs. There are no dues, but occasional collections are taken up when money is needed to repair the instruments.

This young men's association maintains formal relationships with the older people from Kouroussa who live in Bamako. Occasionally, they make gifts of food to the elders, for instance, when they have gotten money from their performances. The association usually performs for the private entertainment of its members. Sometimes it is invited by natives of Kouroussa to a marriage or a circumcision. In such cases, the host must make a gift of money to the association (up to twenty-five hundred francs when it is a rich party). When one of the members of the association marries, a dance is organized for him, but no collection is made for his benefit.

The *dunūba* was very active in February, 1962. It performed nearly every Sunday afternoon in the large empty area between Dravéla and Bolibana, but before a small audience. The band consists of one *dunūba* made of a large oil drum, a single *jēbe* but no horns as in Kouroussa. The dancers (about half a dozen when I saw them) enter dressed up in European clothes—ordinary slacks or blue jeans and shirts. Only the leader wears the large baggy pants, and only he carries a small ax in his hand. Each dancer wears the traditional bandeau and holds in his hand a supple stick of wood or a riding whip. The dancers start walking around the dance ground or *bara*, a large circle more than thirty meters in diameter, with long, fast, stiff strides, but they do not whip each other. A few young men, bare to the midriff, occasionally strike their own backs, but mildly.

Obviously, here the traditional folklore is carried over only to a small degree, and usually without knowledge of its meaning. The dance is performed independently of the traditional occasions. The steps and figures are respected, but formally. The painful whipping is of course avoided, as it cannot be repeated week after week. Furthermore, the absence of girls does not encourage the dancers.[13] The *dunūba* dance has changed from a ceremony to mere entertainment.

The association is still organized, however, on the age-set system, and it is in this respect that it must fit itself into a larger village-like society and that young men continue to pay tribute to old men. The leadership is still founded on age; the actual recruitment is strictly limited to people from a definite area.

This link with the traditional folklore is closely related to poverty and illiteracy. As in the *Jarawara*, the regional rural origin combines with low social status. Indeed, the maintenance of the old form of association, the age-set system, and with it, the submissiveness to the elders, is in danger of keeping the members of such associations in a stagnant conservatism. The effort by the U.S.–R.D.A. to maintain regional folklore while educating the youth in such organizations as the *Pionniers* derives from the perception of this danger.

Sogonĩ-kũ

Sogonĩ-kũ (*sogo*, game; *ni*, diminutive; *kũ*, head) is a dance of masks that comes from the area of Bougouni, a town located two hundred kilometers south of Bamako on a main road to Ivory Coast. For many years, *barañini* (seasonal workers) have come from this area into Bamako. By now a great proportion are permanently settled in town. They are either

---

[13] In 1959, to celebrate Independence, a great *dunũba* was organized by the ward head of Missira, himself a Manĩka from Kouroussa. Every native from the area was present, and according to witnesses, the whipping was very rough.

Bamana from the large Samaké clan, or Fulāke from the Wasulu, populated by sedentarized Fulani and *Numu*-like people.

A Bougouni dance association made up mostly of seasonal workers was reported to have existed in the fifties. In December, 1962, a friendly association of natives from the Bougouni area was reconstituted, with its main purpose "to give them an opportunity to get acquainted and to keep in contact." The initiative was taken by the present president of the association, S.S., a clerk at the *Société Nationale des Transports* and a militant member of the R.D.A.–Niaréla *sous-section,* who contacted several friends from his home town. An elder, son of a previous *Chef de Canton* in Bougouni, who had settled in Médina-Coura before the war and who used to shelter the migrants, was appointed as the *tõ-tie-koroba* (great old man of the *tõ*). They collected money among themselves to buy the instruments and masks and to make gifts to the musicians. Bougouni natives were notified through friends or *griots.* Soon there were more than one hundred members. The entrance fee and monthly dues were set at one hundred francs for men and fifty francs for women. The association is not, according to the president, restricted to people from Bougouni. Actually seven members are said to be from other parts of the country. There is, of course, no tribal discrimination, since Bougouni is an inter-ethnic town. The average age of the members is between thirty-five and forty. Many of them are married and join with their wives. The board consists of ten members: seven live in the ward of Médina-Coura, two live in Missira, and one lives in Niaréla. Four of the board members are petty public servants, one is a male nurse, one a small shopkeeper, one a tailor, one an oil pump attendant, two are laborers, and the last one is the son of a wealthy carrier. The members at large are more disseminated, but seem to polarize around the section to which they first migrated. On the other hand, the mask dancers themselves are younger men between fourteen and twenty, who were born in Bougouni and live temporarily in town as seasonal workers, sometimes unemployed.

The association has no mutual aid purpose, not even in relation to marriage. Its main function is to organize dances either on invitation or on special occasions when the group chooses to honor someone. The first performance of the association was organized in honor of the mayor of Bamako, the next one for the ward headman, and the third for the *tõ-tie-koroba*. These performances followed the custom of the village young men's associations, while gaining at the same time semi-official recognition. The association received five further invitations between December, 1962, and March, 1963. The inviting party must offer fifteen hundred francs and ten kola nuts when the performance takes place in the vicinity of Médina-Coura, and two thousand francs and twenty kola nuts otherwise. The money is used to secure the drums, skins, lamps, benches, and also the masks, which are made in Bougouni by local blacksmiths, as well as to reward the musicians, the dancers, and the singer.

The *tõ* meets once a week, on Saturday evenings, to collect the dues, decide on necessary purchases, report on the expenses, and set the date of the next performance. Women have a committee of their own, but they do not debate with the men. They are informed of the board's decisions and formulate their remarks afterward.

This type of dance was described by M. Prouteaux (1929) in relation to the *Wara de Bougouni*, a tilling society of young men who worked on the fields of village people who agreed to offer a sheep, a chicken, and two meals or twenty-five francs to the young workers. According to Prouteaux, there was no limitation to *wara* membership, which extended to both sexes. Girls were teamed with young men, whom they waited on while work was in progress.[14] Prouteaux mentions five kinds of masks: the *nama* (hyena), the *gõ* (monkey), the *bala* (porcupine), the

---

[14] This society is very close to what is called the *sãsani-tõ*, a generic name for several mask dances of the Bamana. Some are called *ci-wara, ci-nama,* or *gõsõ*. It is possible that Prouteaux has given to the Bougouni tilling association the name of *wara* that he knew from another area and understood as the generic name for *sãsani-tõ*.

misi (buffalo),[15] and several *sogonī-kū*. When the *wara* is called together, *nama* runs around the village to gather the members. After the work is accomplished and the big meal offered by the host has been eaten, the *tō* gives a performance for the entire village, during which various masks come in succession to execute a kind of mimed dance: the hyena, who is looking for his lost wife; the monkey, who gives his children a piece of iron to forge, plaits the hair of his wife, or pretends to be a marabout and a healer; and lastly the *sogonī*, who come one by one to perform tumbling dances. Here one can recognize some features of the *Koteba,* the traditional farcical theater which is found in the Bamana countries of the north.

The Bamako association has kept the essential features of the Bougoni dance but has simplified them. The farcical aspects of the performance have practically disappeared. There are only four masks instead of five, and a single *sogonī-kū.* The band consists of two drums: a *jēbe* and a *gāgā*.[16] Here the four masks are the *nama, gō, sigi* and *sogonī-kū.* The first three masks are mimicked imitations of the animals. During the performance of the buffalo, a confederate plays the part of a frightened hunter. The *sogonī-kū* performs acrobatics, while a woman sings tales of the unforgotten heroes, such as Samory, whose terrible deeds spread terror in the Bougouni country. Between the appearances of the masks young men and even children of the association step in to perform *yayoba,* an acrobatic dance of jumps, somersaults, or *entrechats.* The women's role is limited to singing. They sit close to the drummers, clapping their hands and repeating in chorus the leading verses of a traditional stock of songs.

The *Sogonī-kū,* unlike the previous associations, is not or-

---

[15] *Misi* actually means "cow." Buffalo is translated by *sigi.*

[16] The *jēbe* is a large drum, nearly a meter high and fifty centimeters in diameter, in the general shape of an egg cup. The lower part is firmly held between the legs, while the drum is beaten with palms and fingers. Three vibrating plates with small iron rings loosely attached all along the edges are set vertically on the side of the drum. The *gāgā* is a smaller cylindrical drum with skin on both ends, about fifty to sixty centimeters long and twenty-five centimeters in diameter. It is held below the arm and beaten with a curved stick.

ganized along village age-set patterns. The tendency is to imitate the European hierarchy with *président, vice-président, secrétaire,* and *trésorier.* There is a clear social distinction between the members of the association, who are also the spectators, and the performers. The first are settled people, not even necessarily born in Bougouni country, middle-aged, and married. Economically they hold permanent salaried jobs. The dancers are young men, seasonal workers, and unmarried. The *sogoni* dancer and the woman singer live in an outlying section of the town and must be fetched to come perform in Médina-Coura. Watching the mask has become a recreation for the city dwellers—a pretext for entertainment and a convenient way to celebrate family events. But their pleasure is that of the spectator, not of the participant. The traditional patronage of younger dancers coming from the bush by their elders living in the city might easily become here a kind of paternalistic attitude.

Furthermore, as we shall see more clearly in the *segu-ka-bara,* a mixed membership of married people raises new problems not found in the associations of single men that we have considered so far.

Segu-ka-bara (the Drums from Ségou)

The *segu-ka-bara* is the present name of a dance which is said to belong to the Coulibaly Massasi, the Bamana clan that reigned over the Kaarta from the seventeenth to the nineteenth century. The dance came to Ségou after El Hadj Omar defeated the Massasi. Many of the Massasi migrated to Ségou, the capital of the other Bamana kingdom. After the French conquest, Archinard installed a Massasi on the throne of Ségou, but this ruler soon became so unpopular that he was removed and replaced by a Diara Ngolosi, a member of the Ségou dynasty. A great many Massasi left Ségou on this occasion to return to the Kaarta or settle in other towns. They took their dance along with them—the *bara,* which came to be known as the *segu-ka-bara.* In addition, many people who remained for a time in Ségou (now the main administrative center of the Office du Niger) brought the dance into the various places where they happened to live later.

During the years prior to the last war, the *segu-ka-bara* was still a prestigious dance, quite representative of the traditional aristocratic social structures. In San, for instance, the drummers were either *wolo-so, somono,* or *ñamakala,* and the performance was divided into several dances restricted to men, women, or *wolo-so.* The men of noble descent (*horō*) performed first, wearing their best and richest embroidered *glokiba,* a tarboosh Arabian leather sandals, and holding in their hands the most essential article of the dance: the *bara* or cane, the former insignia of the Bamana king. The *bara* was made of rare and exotic wood, sometimes adorned with sculptured ivory. When the dancer presented himself on the ground, his friends came to him and raised his arms or poured money over him for his *griots.* The dancer demonstrated his skill by spinning and twirling round, squatting down and getting up, kicking one sandal up in the air, letting it fall on its sole while he turned around, and stepping back into it in a single continuous motion. Parading and challenging was just as important as dancing. Through conventional gestures and motions of the cane, the dancer described and pointed at a man in the crowd and challenged him to come to the *bara* and give as much money to his *griots* as the dancer had given to his own. The challenged one, for fear of losing his prestige, had to comply. If he was challenged several times during the performance, he was forced to borrow money from his kinsmen, his mother, or his friends. It is said, however, that such costly challenges were alleviated by an agreement made with the *griots* to the effect that part of the money and gifts were returned afterward.

The *segu-ka-bara,* as I have seen it in Bamako, is a tepid version of the San dances as described above by witness.

At least two different *segu-ka-bara* associations existed in Bamako at the time of this investigation. The striking fact is that the members are not people of high social standing. It was, in fact, very difficult to find out the actual trades of the members. The president of one association was said to be a merchant, but we discovered that he was actually a painter. We were told that the vice-president was employed at the wood-cutting plant, but we were not told in which capacity, although one of his wives said that he was a *bandit bele bele* (*bele bele,* very big). We discovered that the other officers of the association worked at various odd jobs and lived in banco houses, without electricity, in the midst of poor compounds. Only one of the officers, a customs official, lived in a durable modern house. Most were illiterate and hardly spoke French. Among the regular professions of the officers, we noted, besides the customs official, one mason and one policeman. In sharp contrast with the poverty of the lodgings was the wealth of the clothing exhibited during the dance. All these men wore glorious *gloki-ba,* embroidered on the chest, and large Arabian sandals. But only a few had a cane; most held instead a piece of wood or a scarf.

There are three kinds of drums: the *cu* is a huge drum of about sixty-five centimeters in diameter, which is made of a large calabash and hangs from the waist of the drummer. The drum is beaten with both hands and gives a loud, grave tone. The *cu* is traditionally played by *wolo-so* people, but I have seen officers of the association, known to be *horõ,* play it for their enjoyment during a dance, although this, I was told, is not proper. The *gelegelebani* is a drum in the shape of the frustum of a cone, about seventy centimeters high and twenty-five centimeters in diameter. It is held between the legs and beaten with a straight, thin, hard stick and with the fingers of the other hand. The sound is very clear and fast. There might be as many as three *gelegelebani* in the band. The *gãgã,* which has been described in relation to the *sogonĩ-kũ,* is played by a *jeli* or a man of any condition. If there is a *tamani*[17] player present (they are always *jeli*) he may join the band.

---

[17] The *tamani* is a smaller drum made in the shape of two frustrums of a cone joined at their smaller ends, about fifty centimeters long and less than twenty centimeters in diameter. Both ends are covered by skins which are linked together by tightening ropes running from one end of the drum to the other, so that when the drum is held under the armpit, a slight pressure of the arm stretches the skins and alters the tone. The drum is beaten with a curved stick.

During performances, which take place in the street, a table and a few arm chairs are set on one side of a street for the officers, under a large Malian flag stretched along the wall. Benches are set across the street, blocking traffic. The band sits opposite the officers, and a group of women, the singers, sit on one side in between. The *commissaire*, with a ribbon the color of the flag across his chest, holds a small stick and waves it at the children who threaten to invade the dancing ground.

The performance is divided, according to the tradition, into men's, women's, and *wolo-so*'s dances. The men come in one at a time to the rhythm of the *tie-dunu* (drumming of the men). The first volunteer steps into the circle and starts walking around slowly, while his friends come out to congratulate him before he begins whirling and bouncing. Except for the *jeli* of the association, whose dance was the closest to that described above, I did not see any dancer performing in his *gloki-ba*. In between men's and women's dances, young men step in to perform acrobatics very close to what we called *yayoba* in relation to the *sogonī-kū*. Most of these young men are said to be *wolo-so* or *bara-ñini*.

The women's dances are also different from those that must have made up the former *bara*. Few of the young women know the proper steps; most dance some kind of *gūbe* instead. More often, when the *muso-dunu* (the drumming of the women) is beaten, older women offer themselves to the applause of their friends, who lay scarves at their feet or stuff money in their headdresses to be distributed later to the musicians.

Next the *wolo-so-dunu* (drumming of the *wolo-so*) sounds. The tradition of the ancient aristocratic society is that people of slave condition must perform grotesque and obscene dances for the enjoyment of their masters. Many *wolo-so* still accept their condition and volunteer for such performances. Unlike the *horō*, *wolo-so* of both sexes can dance together. The man pulls the upper part of his wide *kurusi* over his belt to simulate a sex organ and makes ludicrous contortions. The woman's favorite gesture is alternately to put her left hand on her nape and her other to her buttock, then the right to the nape and the left one on the sex organs. The *wolo-so* assume forbidden or undignified postures, and there is much laughter from the audience.

In between the dances the musicians, still beating their drums, come to salute the leaders and the guests to collect money.

The *bara* proper is the last part of the performance. The officials in their beautiful *gloki-ba,* guests, and other people of the association who have not danced before, along with all the men of the previous dances, walk around whirling a stick—or more often a scarf—around their heads. During the parade, friends and kin step forward to hold up the arms of the men they want to honor and slip money into their headdresses. Some women walk beside the men, giving the false impression that men and women dance together.

The *Segu-ka-bara* association is said to have existed before World War II. Today it has sixty-five members—thirty-seven men and twenty-eight women—of whom only fifteen are from Ségou. Among the other members, we find people from various areas and places to which the *segu-ka-bara* has been exported. Many are first-generation settlers, married to Bamako women. Most of the members live in Niaréla and Médina-Coura.

There are seven officers of the association: *président, sous-président,* two *commandants,* one *juge,* and two *commissaires.* Actually, the association functions mainly as a *société de mariage.* Members have the opportunity of mobilizing the *bara* to perform at their kinsmen's weddings. From this point of view the features of the dance are twofold. The dance provides entertainment for the dancers and onlookers, and it gives the family an opportunity to receive congratulations from kin and friends in a formal manner. The pleasure that people get from the *bara* performance is enhanced by the celebration involved.

Members pay one hundred francs to join and fifty francs monthly. When one of them celebrates a family event, a collection is made for his benefit. He receives twenty-five hundred francs for a wedding, one thousand francs for a baptism, and less for a circumcision. No provisions are made in case of death.[18] Whoever invites the association to perform offers kola nuts, cigarettes, and refreshments. He must also pay the musicians, in addition to the money which is given to them during the performance, either directly or through the dancers.

During the dry season of 1963, the association was especially active. It met several weeks in a row, first greeting each leader at his home and afterward performing on invitation. Even so, it gave the feeling of an ephemeral surge of activity, common in many associations when they are first established or during periods of revival.

At the time of our investigation, the main problem was to unify the two existing *bara* associations. Discussions were in progress, and the president of the second association had been invited to a performance of the other. But no decisions had been made at the time of our departure.

In spite of its name, the *Segu-ka-bara* is hardly what can be called a regional association. In Bamako, recruitment centered about two wards rather than around ethnic origin. From this point of view, the association is more adapted to urban conditions than any of the others we have discussed.

On the other hand, it is significant as an assessment of social prestige inside traditional aristocratic patterns. Through *Segu-ka-bara*, common people imitate their former masters and sovereigns. The leaders of the association dress well (in sharp contrast with their poor dwellings); they sit apart and well in view during performances; they donate money; they parade with a symbol of sovereignty in their hands and offer themselves to homage and compliments. The organization of the dancing still emphasizes social distinctions between nobles and slaves.

But the dance is performed today by wage earners, small public agents, or unemployed people, not by aristocrats. People

---

[18] The other *bara* association mentioned circumcision as the most common event celebrated by them.

of various conditions, including *ñamakala* and even *wolo-so,* are on an equal footing. When *wolo-so* pay their dues like the other members, they do not perform the grotesque dances, and they participate in the honorable parade. This apparent democratization is more the result of confusion between ancient and modern values than of a deliberate move toward eradication of old social inequalities. That point is proved by the fact that old-fashioned types of *wolo-so* are still laughed at when performing their buffoon dances.

The *Segu-ka-bara* is also an "honorable" way to resist Islamization by retaining old Bamana values. We noted that most of the leaders did not practice the Islamic religion; many do not fast during the Ramadan, nor do they abstain from alcoholic beverages.

Members of the *Segu-ka-bara* tend to look to ancient values as a way for promotion within a limited and backward present social sphere, while at the same time the descendants of their royal models are giving up those very customs in order to adopt a more modern pattern of urban life.

As in the *Sogoñi-kũ,* the majority of the members are married. The young bachelors' role is, as in the bush, to entertain their elders. To this extent we see here a more complete reconstruction of village life and society than in the young men's associations built on age-set models, without membership of the elders. But it leads to new problems: the people brought together in the midst of a larger milieu form an in-group and hence create among themselves a feeling of intimacy in relation to the outside society. Relationships between the sexes in such surroundings are bound to be more intimate, and it is known that these associations soon become the scene of intrigues. Therefore, written and unwritten rules exist to prevent unfortunate complications. Fines or expulsion of both parties are the usual punishments for courting between married people or adultery within the association. We shall see that the rules regulating sex relationships are practically the opposite in the city associations of young people.

Ambiance

The most sumptuous and artistic shows offered in the streets by a Bamako association are undoubtedly the marriage celebrations of *Ambiance,* the association of people of caste, or *jeli-tõ.*

When *jeli-tõ* was first registered under this name in 1956, it numbered forty-eight men and thirty-three women. It was, according to the statutes, a mutual aid society offering assistance in marriages, baptisms, circumcisions, and deaths. Members were of modest social position. The president and two other officers were tailors. Two more officers were secondhand dealers, while the remainder declared themselves to be musicians or artists by trade, i.e., still acted as the traditional *griots.* The entrance fee was set at 100 francs; there were no monthly dues, but a collection was made of 250 francs and 100 francs respectively in case of marriage or birth (dues for the other events were not mentioned in the bylaws). In 1963 the *jeli-tõ* had changed its name to *Association des Artistes du Mali, l'Ambiance.* By then it had about three hundred members, and it had become a powerful association of national scope, with some of its officers drawn from the highest social spheres.

Recruitment was directed toward *ñamakala* of all kinds, from anywhere in Mali. Although they were often referred to by the generic terms of *jeli,* they were in fact also *numu* and, to a less extent, *garãke, fune,* and *dabo.* (The *dabo* are a caste of genealogists for the *jawabe,* a Fula fraction.) Today most of the members are *Manĩka, Kasõke,* and *Sonĩke.* Membership, however, is not restricted to people of caste, and *horõ* are gladly accepted, and are found mostly among the *muso-mise.* *Jõ, wolo-so,* and foreigners may join also, and some actually do.

The members of the *tõ* are divided into four groups according to traditional definitions of age and sex: the *tie-koroba* (old men), the *tie-dẽmise* (adult men; *dẽ,* cadet; *mise,* small); the *muso-koroba* (older women), and the *muso-dẽmise* or *muso-mise* (married women). The *dẽmise* group of men and women is often referred to as *"Ambiance"* proper. Each group has its own officers, but the *tie-koroba,* of course, rank above all the others.

The *jeli kũ-tigi-koroba* (head of the elder *jeli; kũ,* head) is a professional *griot* of Manĩka origin. He has been chosen both because he stands as the oldest and because he is one of the few men entitled to perform the *jãjõ,* the warriors' dance, reserved for those who have accomplished glorious deeds in war or on the hunt. The *jeli kũ-tigi-cini* (smaller headman; *cini,* small, inferior); was chosen "among those who can live in society, get along with people, and settle disputes," i.e., for his sociability and ability as a judge. He is a *gesere* (Sonĩke *griot*) by birth, and a high public servant working in the cabinet of a ministry. He is assisted by a former member of the same cabinet.

The entrance fees amount to 250 francs. There are no dues, but collections are made in case of celebrations or deaths in members' families. In case of a marriage, members of both sexes must give 250 francs if the bride is to be married for the first time or 100 francs if she is divorced or widowed. At baptism members give 100 francs, and 250 francs are given in case of death. Sessions are said to take place at the house of the *tie-koroba-kũ-tigi* once every month.

The association performs on various occasions, sometimes at the invitation of one of the members to celebrate a familial event, sometimes on its own volition to honor one of its prominent members. It also organizes dances to celebrate national or political events such as the meeting of the U.S.–R.D.A. Convention in September, 1962. Actually the association is the marriage society par excellence, and it meets essentially on such occasions. During the dry season of 1963, it celebrated the marriages of several members' relatives, sometimes several weeks in a row. The celebration of a marriage lasts a full week, during which the association is expected to perform every night. However, when marriages took place in close succession, it became too much of a burden to respect this rule.

I attended several of these magnificent performances and shall give a synthesized description, since they follow a fairly fixed pattern. The wealth of the association is demonstrated by its equipment. The afternoon before the evening performance, low-ranking *ñamakala* [19] of the association prepare a large space in front or near the house of the person who issued the invitation. They drive poles into the ground around a square, and hang a chain of electric lights on all four sides. Loud speakers set at every corner amplify the music of the orchestra. The show begins at night, after dinner.

The orchestra is composed of instruments which are typical of the *ñamakala:* the *Manīka kora,* [20] the *balani,* [21] the *jeli-dunu,* [22] the *jeli dunūba,* [23] and the *tamani,* [24] to which are added electric guitars. The *dunūba* players hold in their left hand a *gereñe* (large bell), which they strike on an iron ring slipped around the thumb.

The musicians take their places on one side of the square. They are led by I. Sisoko, a *griot* of great talent, a renowned composer and leader of the *Ensemble National* (National Orchestra). Behind the musicians sit the *muso-koroba,* and on the opposite side the *Ambiance* women. The *tie-koroba* are seated in armchairs facing the group of women singers; the *tie-dēmise* squat on mats, sometimes before the older men, sometimes in a corner. Everyone is dressed in sumptuous traditional garments. Both groups of women wear their own uniform *monrovia*—a large stole of gauze or light material decorated with gold or silver design—and expensive jewelry. The above four groups always sit separately according to sex and age. A master of ceremonies circulates among the groups, encouraging the mem-

[19] They are apparently *ñamakala* without either a modern education or the artistic ability necessary to live off rich families.

[20] Twenty-one strings are stretched on two parallel rows between a sound box made of half a calabash covered with cow hide and a handle stuck through the box. Two smaller sticks on both sides of the handle are used to hold the instrument between the last three fingers of both hands while the strings are pinched between the thumbs and the forefingers. The instrument is one meter, ten centimeters high or more, and it is made by specialized *griots*.

[21] Wooden xylophone of smaller size than the one described in note 8, above.

[22] Cylindrical drums with skins stretched on both ends, hanging from the shoulder, and beaten with a curved stick.

[23] Identical drums such as the ones above but larger and laid on the ground.

[24] See the description given in relation to the *segu-ka-bara.*

bers of the association to dance by throwing a scarf at them, or urging the women to sing.

The performance is a succession of songs and dances. The songs originate in various parts of the country, mostly in Kita and Kayes. They are performed by women singers of repute—some of them radio stars—who may come from far away to celebrate a friend's wedding. Dances are performed alternately by men and women, but the two sexes never dance together. The men's dance is an individual performance. On coming to the ground, the dancer walks slowly back and forth to give his fellows an opportunity to come and greet him. Kinsmen of the groom and bride often restrict their show to this first parade. Others, after being greeted, perform a dance which resembles what the *bara* formerly must have been. The women's favorite dances are the *diãsa*, the marriage dance, which is also said to be the dance of the *jeli* women from Kasõ. *Tage*, the dance of the Sonĩke blacksmith women, is more difficult but performed by women of all conditions. In the midst of the performance, the women of the association partici- pate in a formal parade, slowly moving around the dancing ground, cheered by the crowd. The show often ends with the performance of a kind of verse chronicle called *fasa*, sung by a famous *griot* accompanied by a *kora* player.

These sumptuous and expensive performances sometimes take place several nights in a row, lasting from 8:30 or 9:00 to 11:00 or midnight. One of the most anticipated features of the celebration is the speech of Garãke Mamu—Mamu the Cob- bler. He is considered the best speaker of the *ñamakala;* he takes the floor at almost every *Ambiance* performance to con- gratulate the bride and groom and their families and to an- nounce the gifts. Many of his speeches are witty—and politi- cal.

Ambiance is a thorny problem for the U.S.–R.D.A. Overtly the association has completely rallied to the party's position. In a speech printed in the official paper, *L'Essor,* on September 15, 1962, the *Premier Vice Président* (the *tie-dẽmise ku-tigi*) ex- pressed it without ambiguity: "Les artistes . . . sont avant tout des militants et des responsables politiques convaincus de la justesses des options de l'US–RDA et qui tous militent activement dans leurs comités de quartier respectif." When the members of *Ambiance* organize an outstanding celebration, they never fail to invite the *Président de la République* or some of his representatives. At a performance in September, 1962, the closest associate of Modibo Keita, J. M. Kone, sat in the tribune of honor along with the *Secrétaire General du Parti* and the President of the National Assembly. On other occasions, the *Haut Commissaire à la Jeunesse et au Sport*, brother of the *Président de la République* has attended. He was reminded on one of these visits that he had been named Musa after a *jeli*, a beloved friend of his father. In the same speech, Mamu undertook to explain the political functions of the *ña-makala* in the new regime: they actively participate in the *construction nationale* through highly effective pro-government propaganda, praising and explaining the leaders and the party's objectives.

Several conservative currents, however, can be found in the *jeli-tõ*. Culturally, it tends to maintain a beautiful and valuable folklore, an endeavor which has always been encouraged by the regime. This preservation is not, however, the exclusive contribution of the *tõ*, since such official institutions as the *Pionniers*, the *Centre Culturel*, and the Ministry of Information are actively and efficiently working along the same lines. On the other hand, the *jeli-tõ* closely binds the artistic background of the association to the permanency of the castes. *Ambiance* leaders, instead of working toward dissolution of castes, emphasize their usefulness and value, and assign to them specific functions in the modern society. This conservative position constitutes a refusal to eradicate the ancient forms of social inequality, in opposition to the official socialist doctrine which advocates a society in which all individuals are equal without consideration of birth; where social promotion is founded on work and not on the activities of a court; where marriage is the result of free choice and no longer an instrument of power for the elders or a diplomatic deal completed

112 Urbanization of an African Community

through shrewd intercessors. All this would mean a society without *ñamakala*.[25]

As it is, the preservation of the folklore, when it is associated with the maintenance and the promotion of the castes, stands as a social background for a conservative political movement whose adherents reach far beyond the ancient social structures.

Associations for Social Promotion

The Bara

Although the *segu-ka-bara* is still performed as a folk dance today, between 1935 and 1956 it found modern expression in the several *bara* associations which existed in every ward in Bamako, and whose day has now passed. This kind of association has disappeared, but it remains important in the social history of Bamako as a preliminary to the present youth associations. It is a link between regional traditional associations and modern associations.

The urban Bamako *bara* is different from the *segu-ka-bara* in at least two respects. First, it is organized on the basis of the ward, inside a broad network of similar ward associations. The first *bara* is reported to have been created in Dar-Salam as early as 1935; by 1945, seven *bara* existed, one in every ward. When three new wards were created in 1953, they formed their own dance associations. And second, the *bara* is an association of young unmarried people, most of them born in town.

The bulk of our information concerns the Dravéla *bara*, during the period of its most intense activity, from 1947 to 1954. It was, perhaps, one of the most brilliant of the *bara* associations since it seems to have left vivid memories.

B.T., our main informant, joined the Dravéla *bara* after he had left the *gūbe*, in 1941, when he was thirteen years old. There were, he said, no membership restrictions on the basis of the traditional social differentiations.[26] At the time of its great-

---

[25] In several of the plays performed by the young people from the *Centres Culturels*, the theme of forbidden marriages with people of caste or *wolo-so* is treated and bitterly criticized. The *ñamakala* (of the traditional kind, of course) are often shown as the willing instruments of the prohibitions.

[26] Neither the *ñamakala* nor the *wolo-so* paid the dues, however, as "one does

est expansion, the *bara* had about 120 members of both sexes between 14 and 18 years of age, most of whom lived in the ward, though residence was not, theoretically, taken into consideration.

The association was led by five officers: the *président*, the *vice-président*, the *commissaire*, the *trésorier*, and the *almamy*. The girls had their own officers—the *présidente*, the *vice-présidente*, the *commissaire*, and the *griote*—who were, however, only a consultative and informal body.

There was no periodical election. The leaders were nominated by the officers and acclaimed during a *tō-sigi* whenever the need occurred. The first president was a young Manīka bachelor, born outside Bamako and a "boy" (domestic servant) by trade. He was elected because he was a good speaker and got along well with everyone. He held office for five years, until he left town. From 1946 to 1948, the president was a Suraka clerk in a European store, again a bachelor, who later left to go to Mecca and became a marabout. After him another Toure [27] was elected, a bachelor born in Bamako, not the oldest, but trustworthy. He was a butcher by trade. In 1952 he was replaced by our informant, a Touré from the Dravé family, who had been *commissaire* since 1941. He was twenty-four at that time.

Besides the board, the association had its *tō-jeli*, either a *griot* by birth or a *wolo-so*, but never a *horō*, as happens in the *gūbe*. The *tō-jeli* fulfilled the functions of *dalamina* during meetings and of master of ceremonies during performances. He was also responsible for the material arrangements of the celebrations. Four *polisi* were appointed by the officers to execute decisions in regard to discipline, as expressed in the written rules of the association.

---

not take money from these people." They were in charge of the organization of the dances and celebrations.

[27] Touré is the *jamu* (or patronym) for clans, families, or people who might have been Sonīke originally but who are considered today to be of Moorish (Suraka) descent and Moslem. As we know, the Touré were one of the two leading clans in Bamako, but many people who bear the *jamu* do not necessarily belong to the original clan. The Dravé call themselves Touré.

In 1941 the entrance fees were twenty-five francs; weekly dues, paid every Friday evening, were the same amount for both boys and girls. There was, in addition, an exit fee, payable when a member wanted to quit the association, which was extremely high—five hundred francs, plus one hundred kola nuts and a sheep. The *tõ* met formally every Monday and Friday evening. When a member could not pay his dues, the *polisi* were instructed to take away his or her shoes or head-dress. Dances took place every Wednesday and Saturday night and on the first and third Sundays of the month. The *tabaski,* as we shall see below, was the occasion of a special celebration.

The musicians were chosen from among the best players, without any other consideration. They played two kinds of drums: one *cu* and four *gelegelebani.* The musicians (and the *ñamakala*) paid no dues, and they were occasionally given the price of their cigarettes. The girls of the *tõ* sang in chorus, the best of them being the leading singers. The performance was divided in successive parts, roughly as in the *segu-ka-bara,* although the steps were not completely identical. The *bara* has a stock of traditional songs which are, according to my inform-ants, proper to the *bara* from Ségou. The few that I collected are mostly related to the *tie-dunu,* and they speak of war, wealth, and women. The lyrics are in Bamana.

In addition to the regular dances, marriages were occasions for extra performances. When a girl or a boy from the *bara* got married, it was customary for the kinsmen to offer to the association a dish of *moĩni,*[28] two dishes of rice, twenty kola nuts, and fifty francs. These gifts were offered when the *bara* escorted the bride or the groom to their homes on the Thursday before the wedding. On the following Saturday night they performed at the groom's gate, and on the Sunday afternoon and night they danced before the girl's home. Besides dancing and honoring the newlyweds, no other contributions were made by the association.

The *tabaski* was the occasion of a special celebration and of

[28] Meal made of millet flour rolled into small lumps and boiled in water with sugar, lemon, or tamarind and usually eaten at breakfast.

friendly contacts between the various *bara* in town. In the afternoon a first *bara* dance was performed, and in the evening the association put on a dinner party in the European fashion. Thirty to forty tables were set in the street with plates and silverware (although it is still common, in all social circles, to eat with the hands). The food was paid for from the common fund and prepared by the female members. Tables were, in principle, occupied by couples, but anyone could sit alone at a friend's table. The dinner lasted several hours, from 9:00 or 11:00 P.M. until 3:00 or 4:00 in the morning. Between courses the guests danced modern European dances to the music of an accordion. The *bara* proper started at about 4:00 A.M. and lasted one or two hours. The next Sunday, the several *bara* in town invited each other to perform together. The host association offered drinks, kola nuts, and cigarettes to their guests. Relations between the various *bara* were good, and they also danced together on occasions other than the *tabaski*.

Relations between girls and boys within the association were regulated according to a special institution that we shall find even more highly developed in the *gŭbe*. Every boy was supposed to have a girl friend, a *bara-sŭguru*, but the choice of the partner was made by the girls. Each time the association had four or five new girls, a special meeting was called to give them an opportunity to select their *bara-kamele*. The girls were given a scarf to throw on the boy they elected; choice was restricted to those who did not have a *sŭguru* already, since "monogamy" was the rule. The selection was supposed to be final, and if the girl wanted to quit the boy she had chosen, she was compelled to give one hundred kola nuts, five hundred francs, and a sheep. Sometimes she was also beaten up by the *polisi*. The boy who wanted to repudiate a girl paid a lower fine.

The Dravéla *bara* disappeared gradually. The older members, says B.T., got married, and the younger ones were attracted by other kinds of entertainment: the ball, the movies, the bicycle, and the clubs, as we shall see below. By 1959, the association had come to an end.

The *bara* is typical as a transitional type of association. The cultural background, although it has degenerated, is entirely traditional: the dances, the songs, the music, and the instruments all belong to the past civilization, as does the persisting discrimination between *horŏ* and *wolo-so*. But this cultural inheritance is assumed by young unmarried people and not by the rich elderly men and women. While the members of the *Segu-ka-bara* described above patently imitated their former masters, the young people from the *bara* took over from their elders with greater liberty and changed the association into a dynamic and lively institution devoted not to carrying on customs and folklore from an ancient social order, but to adapting to the urban milieu and meeting their new social needs. If the entertainment is still founded on tradition, *bara* members, nevertheless, dance European jive to the sound of an accordion, and once a year adopt European manners and attitudes.

We find this duality again in the organization of the association. Offices, even the "police," are not foreign to the traditional forms of leadership and discipline. There are still a *tŏ-jeli* and a *dalamina* as in most other associations; fines are paid both in money and in kola nuts. But the association recruits on the basis of the ward and thus thinks of itself as opposed to the other *bara* of the city on this ground. Officers boast European titles; girls have special privileges and are a representative body in the midst of the association; they also have the advantage of paying lower fees than the boys and, above all, the freedom to choose their partners.

Many of these features are highly developed in the *gŭbe,* to which we now turn, and on which we shall dwell as the most developed type of transitional urban association and as the last link with the traditional way of life.

The Gŭbe [29]

History of the Gŭbe in Bamako. Among the free entertainments offered in the streets by Bamako associations, one can

[29] To avoid all confusion, it should be stated at once that the Bamako *gŭbe* is different from what Holas describes for Ivory Coast (Holas 1953). It is also

see on week ends, in the afternoon or at night, very young boys and girls performing little ballets to loud and rhythmical beats and yarns.

On one side, sitting in a row, four or five boys between the ages of fourteen and sixteen beat square-shaped drums and a big battery (a round modern beat drum, as found in modern jazz). On the opposite side, girls of about the same age or even younger, some wearing dresses cut from the same fabrics, sing heartily and clap their hands in rhythm. Standing around, the neighbors and the passers-by watch young dancers of both sexes perform complicated figures in the middle of the ring.

Behind this performance stands an association which has its own history in Bamako. Everybody agrees that the *gũbe* probably came from Sénégal, but no one knows exactly when. The word *gũbe* is foreign to any of the languages spoken in Bamako. No one knows where it came from or what it means.[30] However, *gũbe* associations are reported to have existed as early as the thirties. In 1935 they were active in Niaréla, Bagadadji, Ouolofobougou, and Médina-Coura. There were none in Dravéla. In Dar-Salam there was also a *bara,* while the *sabar,* a Wolof inspired folk association, existed alongside the *gũbe* in Bagadadji. But in the ward of Bamako-Coura, three *gũbe* existed together—we shall refer to the one called *Jeunesse de Bamako-Coura.*[31]

The *gũbe* of various city wards were not competitive, since their recruitment was for the most part, though not exclusively, territorially defined. They maintained at that time friendly relationships and used to invite each other to perform together on Sundays. Competition was stronger among *gũbe* from the

---

different from the Dakar *gũbe,* which have been described to me as a kind of quadrille, apparently similar to what Banton describes as the *Ambas Geda* in Freetown (Banton 1957:173). The present study is based on close observation of one recent *gũbe* that we joined, and on reports on two past ones by Bassily Toure and Gaoussou Camara.

[30] One can assume that it comes from the word *compin* (from the English "company") as used in Sierra Leone, for instance, to name the associations at large (Banton 1957:187).

[31] Since another *gũbe* of the same name existed in the fifties, we shall refer to this one as JBC I and to the later one as JBC II.

same ward, as, for instance, among the three that existed in Bamako-Coura. It is reported that they entered into a feud over a girl who left one association to join another without paying the exit fee. Fights sometimes involving thirty to forty youths of both sexes took place in the streets. Hostilities lasted two months, until the father of the girl learned the cause and paid the fee. The *gũbe* boys were also in competition with the debonair college men who came on Saturday nights to flirt with the *gũbe* girls. Insults and fights occurred at these encounters.

During the same period, as we have already mentioned, other similar dance associations existed—the *bara,* described above, and the *sabar.* This last dance, also of Sénégalese origin, was forbidden in 1947 by the *Chef de Canton* because of its alleged lewdness. Some of the figures required that dancers of opposite sexes lie on top of each other or display their private parts. At that time, some of the *sabar* associations, such as the one in Médina-Coura, which were former *gũbe,* reverted to their original form.

In 1954–55, the most famous *gũbe* was the *Royal* from Bagadadji. It was probably the first *gũbe* created after the war. The style had been transformed by then under influences coming from Ivory Coast. The founders of the *Royal* were in fact young merchants (*kalãdẽ*) traveling between Bamako and Abidjan. The leadership was in sympathy with the P.S.P. party, and for this reason a split occurred in 1955 when the R.D.A. partisans left the *Royal* to found the *Triomphe* in the same section of Bagadadji. Tino, the best *latikeli-kela* (drummer), left with his girl, one of the finest dancers, and with them the very popular song he had composed in her honor. Rivalry arose between the two associations, not out of territorial competition, but for political reasons.

Antagonism was severe between the girls of rival associations, who actually opened battle in the main market place, a fight which resulted in several injuries and bruises. Recurrent fights took place every time the girls ran into each other, until the older people complained to the police.

The examples of the *Royal* and the *Triomphe,* however, had stimulated Bamako youth to create other *gũbe* in most wards. It was at that time that *Jeunesse de Bamako-Coura II* was created. All *gũbe* were established with the same rules. They lasted until 1950 when the government undertook to integrate all the youth associations into the party. This endeavor was resented by most *gũbe* members, who left their associations one after the other.

At the time of our investigation, *gũbe* had reappeared. We located three of them—one in Médina-Coura, one in Baga-dadji, and one in Niaréla. We joined the latter association, but it was short-lived. Apparently, the time of the great *gũbe* was over, and youths were more attracted by a new type of association of greater prestige—the clubs, which we shall describe in detail later.

Organization of the Gũbe. From the above data, one can see that the *gũbe* is more competitive and militant than the *bara,* and that it is built along less aristocratic lines. It represents an interesting modernization of the village *flã-tõ,* as well as an awkward search for modern values.

The cases we collected show that the *gũbe* were created by groups of friends who wanted to structure their relationships, and who sought an opportunity to bring into their social reach the girls of their neighborhood and to have a chance to play a leading role among the other boys. If they decided to form a *gũbe,* they looked for adult man of good repute to act as the *tõ-fa,* on the model of the traditional father of the *flã-tõ,* whose duties were mainly to conciliate possible conflicts and to advise the young members. One of his wives, or another woman known to be sympathetic to the young people, was asked to be the *tõ-ba.* Thereafter they selected the officers. Names were suggested, usually by the eldest boy or by the *tõ-ba,* who seemed to enter more assiduously into the daily life of the association than did the *tõ-fa.* The president was customarily the eldest, if he was considered able. Other officers were selected to fit their functions, not necessarily according to age.

In *Jeunesse de Bamako-Coura II* the girls have no board as in the Niaréla *gũbe.* But in the latter, girls, who are under the leadership of the *tõ-ba*, fulfill hardly any actual functions, so that the correspondence between age and rank is nearly complete.

Further recruitment is made from the initial core, usually through co-optation. Every member is proud to bring in a friend or an old acquaintance. Boys or girls from the ward who are considered desirable recruits—because they are rich, talented, or attractive—are approached. Others ask for admission. Their requests are examined at meetings, along with proposals on ways and means to contact certain boys or girls.

Qualifications for membership seem completely divorced from the traditional ones. As was mentioned, *ñamakala* are prized as organizers of the performances, perhaps as drummers, drum makers, dancers, or factotums. But anyone could fulfill these functions. In the early *gũbe*, *ñamakala* did not pay fees or fines; later on whoever was drummer or dancer was exempted, regardless of status.

In the Niaréla *gũbe* the children do not know for certain who was or was not *ñamakala*, although the *jamu* is usually indicative, and they do not seem to care. Indeed, two of the drummers are *numu*, while the *dalamina* is a *horõ*.

Ethnic background is also irrelevant. In the three *gũbe* we studied, the officers were Fulãke, Manĩka, Bamana, and Sonĩke. The above traits are precisely those found in the traditional *flã-tõ*, in which all the boys are mixed, whatever their caste or class. However, here the girls belong to the same association as the boys, although they do not sit among them. They are under the leadership of the *tõ-ba* in a closer way than the boys; they sometimes have their own officers.

There are no written rules about the age of the members, but it is understood that, except for the leaders, only unmarried youths may join.

In the *gũbe* JBC I (1935) the boys were recruited between the ages of twelve and fifteen, some younger; the girls were as young as ten or twelve. The oldest members were officers, since age was the main qualification for responsibilities. Still, they were very young: the president and eldest of all was sixteen, the vice-president was between twelve and thirteen, the others were between twelve and fifteen. After they reached sixteen or seventeen, the members would quit to join the local *bara*.

In JBC II (1955) the officials are older—between twenty-two and twenty-five, the youngest being eighteen.

In Niaréla, the president is about twenty-seven and the secretary twenty-five. The other members are in their teens. The boys are between twelve and eighteen, while the girls are much younger on the average. Small girls under ten sit quietly on benches next to their elders, who are not more than fifteen.

The main qualification to join a *gũbe* is a minimum urban standing. With a few exceptions, the *gũbe* leaders are born in town; in the Niaréla *gũbe*, for example, most of the members were born in Bamako. They were playmates who grew up in the same ward or were educated in the same school. Another requirement for the boys is to have money. Boys with steady jobs or with wealthy parents are welcome: they will be able to pay their fees and various other expenses linked to membership. Beyond these qualifications, some are appreciated as artists and, if they are really wanted as such, may be exempted from fees and recruited from among peasant boys. Girls are preferably pretty and good dancers or singers. In turn, a *dawla-tigi* (good-looking boy with charm) capable of attracting girls is also a good recruit.

The *président* of the JBC I was a mechanic, the other officials were schoolboys. We know already the trade of the board members of JBC II; among the rank and file some were salesmen in Syrian or European shops, others were mechanics, *jula-kalãdẽ*, bicycle salesmen, waiters, schoolboys, and students. People with low-ranking jobs, such as a horse-cart driver, for instance, would not have been admitted.

In the Niaréla *gũbe*, the *président* is a *planton* and the *secrétaire* a taxi driver; others are radio repairmen, *jula-kalãdẽ*, or schoolboys and students; one is an agricultural adviser, and another is the son of a wealthy merchant.

The rules of the various *gũbe* are similar; several features are like those found in the *bara*.

Entrance fees are not very high (twenty-five francs in Niaréla) but dues are collected weekly (twenty-five francs for the boys and fifteen francs for the girls) and amount to comparatively high sums, considering the ages of the members. We shall investigate the problems this raises.

The *gũbe* requires strict discipline from its members. The bylaws make provisions for the following offenses: nonattendance, delays, gossiping, fighting, or calling the president by his name instead of his title.[32] Fines are paid in money and in kola nuts and are often modified to suit the sex and rank of the offender.

In the Niaréla *gũbe*, offenses and fines are as follows:

nonattendance:	10 kola nuts (at 1 for 5 francs)
delay:	10 kola nuts
gossiping:	10 kola nuts
fighting:	100 francs
calling the president by his name:	the fine is set by the board

Girls are fined only five kola nuts, whatever the offense; officers are fined not according to the offense but by rank, whenever "they do something wrong":

président:	200 francs and 40 kola nuts (1 for 5 francs)
secrétaire:	150 francs and 30 kola nuts
vice-président:	50 francs and 10 kola nuts
commissaire:	100 francs

Joining the *gũbe* is a move that the *tõ* tries to make binding. One cannot belong to two *gũbe* at the same time, nor to any similar association, such as a *bara* or a *sabar*. Furthermore, one cannot leave the association without paying an exit fee, lower than in the *bara* (250 francs in Niaréla). However, the collection of these fees is usually difficult and leads to problems, since one leaves the association, in most cases, because of dissent and sometimes bitter resentment.

In the Niaréla *gũbe*, one boy, C., a college student and son of a rich merchant, had been fined for gossiping during the sitting. C., who was older than some of the officers, was vexed to be sanctioned like a common member and stubbornly refused to pay. When the *secrétaire* instructed the *polisi* to take C.'s shoes, as is the rule in such a case, C. left in such anger that the other *polisi*, who was told to stop him at the

[32] There was an old custom in Bamana country not to call the king by his name, nor to pronounce it.

door, simply did not dare to detain him. A friend of C. ran after him, and later the two boys returned. C. was repentant and paid the fine. Many speeches, including one by the *tõ-fa,* were made to celebrate the union of the *tõ* members. Unfortunately, the secretary and another member of the board, who seemed particularly aggressive against C., dwelt on his offenses, causing the disputes to break out again, and C. left angrily for the second time. Before the next *gübe* meeting, a campaign took place, inspired by C.'s friends, to encourage other members to resign, as C. was ready to do: the fees were too high anyway. C.'s resignation took place at the next meeting. He called for the floor and tried to make the occasion as solemn and impressive as possible. First he wanted to read his statement in French, instead of in Bamana, which was always used during the sessions. There was an argument on this point; he was finally allowed to use French. The statement was turgid and full of clichés, borrowed, sometimes in the wrong sense, from administrative jargon. When he was finished speaking, he and his friends were asked to pay the exit fee. Actually the fine was never paid, as his departure was the beginning of the dismembering of the *gübe.* In this case the weakness and low spirit of the association made it impossible to compel the departing parties to pay.

In the *gübe* of the fifties, however, which were a power in the ward, it was more difficult not to pay. Special bodies of strong-armed boys were appointed to look for the offenders in the streets and beat them up.

Belonging to a *gübe* takes a great deal of time. *Tõ-sigi* are held one or two evenings a week, and dancing performances, when the association has vitality, are given as often as twice a week. In addition, rehearsals make a total of three to five meetings during the week.

In Niaréla, the meetings were held in the compound of the *tõ-fa.* Boys and girls sat separately on benches or mats in front of the officers, who were seated on chairs or in armchairs. The officers of the girls were seated among the other girls. The *juge* sat beside the *trésorier* at a table with an exercise book in which the names of the members were listed. The *dalamina* stood in front of him. A *polisi* was at hand holding a small notebook. Another was at the compound *blõ,* checking entrances and preventing exits. The *commissaire* sat among the members.

To open the session the *secrétaire* calls for order. From then on, everybody is supposed to keep quiet and those who do not are recorded by the *polisi* in his notebook. The *juge* calls on each member, whose name is repeated by the *dalamina,* for payment of the dues. This is no routine matter. When a member is unable to pay, he may be given a "credit," sometimes renewable after long discussion, until the next weekly session. If he is already indebted and unable or unwilling to pay, the *secrétaire* decides whether to give the order to the *commissaire* for one of his *polisi* to take the offender's shoes. Therefore some members come without shoes, but only rarely, because it is bad manners. In such cases, however, the *polisi* will be instructed to take away some other garment. Once, a small boy was left in his drawers, shivering in the December cold, until a compassionate friend paid the dues for him.

Fee collection takes a great deal of time. Some boys make a show of it, and so do the *polisi* and the *commissaire* sometimes. When there is verbal resistance—I never saw any physical resistance—the officers take the floor and the discussion becomes general. However, since no one can speak except to the *dalamina,* who repeats the words of the speaker aloud, the discussion remains orderly. After the boys' dues are collected, the girls' turn comes. A few of them pay for themselves, but if a girl is unable to pay, the board calls on her *kamele,* and a repetition of the previous situation occurs: more discussions and more shoes taken away, sometimes from the officers themselves, to the great enjoyment of the assembly.

By then, two hours have passed, and time is nearly up. Still, the fines remain to be paid. The *polisi* comes forward and calls the names of the offenders. They usually protest, and there are more discussions, until they finally agree to pay. When a boy who already has had troubles because of his own dues, his girl's dues, and his own fines is again fined for his *sũguru*'s offenses, it is a merry time indeed.

Once all collections are made, the *trésorier* reports the amount of money collected and the cash balance. If time remains, the assembly discusses the problems of the association, but such discussion is usually tabled until the next meeting, which will not, in principle, be devoted to fee collection.

The second weekly assembly begins, however, in the same way. All the names are called again, and whoever is in debt is invited to pay under the same penalty. Again it takes a great deal of time. Afterward the *tõ* discusses such problems as the purchase of material (benches, lamps, drums, and so forth); the organization of the next dance, or who shall be greeted next by the *tõ*. Amendments to the rules or new regulations are suggested. If the discussion becomes very hot, the *dalamina* is bypassed, and the assembly ends in confusion. However, generally the meetings are quite orderly and the assembly capably solves the problems it has to face, particularly the organization of the dance performances, which requires a minimum of efficient co-ordination.

The *gũbe* performs mostly for its own members (preferably in order of rank), to honor a prominent person in the ward or simply for its own enjoyment. Such performances are called *gũbejo* (*jo*, to greet or to play an instrument).

The *gũbejo* takes place in the street, in the afternoon or at night, before the door of the honored person or at any convenient place. Benches and lamps are brought in by the rank and file under the direction of an officer. Though it is not statutory, boys from castes were, and sometimes still are, considered as the most competent for this kind of work. The band brings the drums, and the host, if there is one, offers the cigarettes and the *jĩjebere* (ginger beer).

Marriages of members are also an occasion for a *gũbejo*. When a boy gets married, the *gũbe* pays for the entertainment and sometimes hires a cornet player. The groom offers cigarettes, *jĩjebere,* and kola nuts. When it is a girl, the various charges are assumed by the girl's *kamele,* unless he had wanted to marry her, in which case the association pays for the entertainment.

Features of the Gũbe Dances. The *gũbe* is a typical dance association, marked by specific features that set it apart from such similar associations as the *sabar* or the *bara*. Many of these distinguishing features are to be found in the instruments and dance steps. In the 1930's and probably until about 1950, the *gũbe* was played on several quadrangular drums of various sizes (called *gũbe ba, tẽtẽ, gũbe-de*). This style spread to Ivory Coast (Holas 1953), where it supported strong Moslem associations, but where it also underwent some stylistic changes, such as the use of a cornet for important occasions, that were eventually brought back to Bamako. By 1954, the drums used were one *jazee* (from the word "jazz"), one *latikeli* ("cutter"), and two or more *pĩpõ*.

The *gũbe* has a stock of songs borrowed from various sources, easily distinguished from the songs of other kinds of associations. Although there undoubtedly have been variations in the tunes since the thirties, these are difficult to spot. A few songs come from the traditional folklore, some as old as the fourteenth century. Most, however, are inspired by modern music, and phrases of Charleston, *rumba,* samba, mambo, conga, and cha-cha can be detected. Lyrics tend to be obtuse, and some have puzzling words; many are related to forgotten events that happened in unknown times to forgotten characters. The meaning of the words, sometimes borrowed from a foreign dialect or from French slang, appears to be of little importance: they are sounds used as support for the tune. As in other types of traditional associations, singing is the business of the girls. When there is no cornet, one or more of them sing the leading verses, which are then repeated by the chorus. The same song is repeated again and again until the leaders introduce a new one.

The steps are even more directly inspired by Western dances than is the music: *rumba,* Charleston, beguine, mambo, and today the cha-cha and merengue, rock-and-roll, and the twist. New steps are more readily adopted than new tunes or rhythms, so that the latest steps are danced to older tunes, apparently without difficulty. Indeed, the word "step" might be deemed inappropriate, because "figure" would better describe the use and transformation of Western dances in the *gũbe* melting pot. Perhaps the most original feature of the *gũbe* is the way in which these figures are used as basic material for an original choreography. *Gũbe* dancing has become a kind of ballet, danced by both sexes, according to a rehearsed pattern. The ballets are numerous and depend on the imagination of the *dõkela* (dancer), a boy with particular talent who invents, rehearses, and leads the figures. Some are choreography; others are acrobatic or humorous skits. The *gŭbe* is a show given for the benefit of neighbors and kinsmen and not exclusively a pastime for its members. There are no couples enfolded into each other's arms, though to the disapprobation of their elders, boys and girls do dance together.

Relationships Between Boys and Girls of the Gŭbe. Particular rules govern relationships between the boys and girls of the *gŭbe*. One purpose of the association is to give the young people from the same ward an opportunity to meet. Knowing this, people are sometimes reluctant to send their daughters to the *gŭbe;* they judge it according to the morality of the *tõ-ba* and *tõ-fa*. But whatever their opinion, it seems that they tolerate it, in fear, perhaps, of appearing to be bad neighbors. They insist, however, on sending small girls along with their elder sisters as chaperones. Hence the large number of small girls found at *gŭbe* meetings. They are accepted into full membership, but they are looked upon with disdain by the older boys, who nickname them *drome-saba* or *drome-fla* (three-to-a-penny or two-to-a-penny).

As in the *bara*, girls are entitled to choose partners, but in a slightly different way. It is reported that in the forties the choice was made at random by the girls, after they had been blindfolded. But since this procedure led to many unfortunate matches, it was abandoned, and girls were given a free choice.

At present, the rules, written or not but common to all *gŭbe,* state that periodically, every three or four months, all the girls renew their choices. On this particularly anguishing day for the boys, each girl is given in turn a scarf to throw on her *kamele*. The rule is that the boy must accept the girl as his *amante* or *tõ-sŭguru*. He can repudiate her later, but in this case he pays a heavy fine. Girls can also quit their *kamele,* even though they chose him, but they pay a lower fine. Several girls can pick the same boy, who must ask for permission from the first *sŭguru* to accept the new ones.

Since the smaller girls are full members, they are entitled—if only for financial reasons—to pick a partner, but after the older girls. They are left with the second-choice boys. The main duty of the *kamele* is to pay his girl's dues and fines if she is unable to do so herself. In turn, the *kamele* is entitled to visit his girl in the evening if he wishes and to take her for walks. If he has several girls he must visit them in turn. The girls' choices are sometimes dictated by feelings, sometimes by self-interest; the danger for a boy who always comes smartly dressed is that he may find himself with a large harem of girls of all ages.

Gũbe courtship does not necessarily lead to matrimony and, as a matter of fact, it is hardly considered in this light, since marriage still depends largely, for the girls, on the parents' choice, a fact that is well known to both parties. The courtship may be partial fulfillment of a wish for freedom and romance. It is also an opportunity to exert one's charm and appeal within the safety of an institutional and limiting organization. The *gũbe* is a milieu in which such relationships can be bounded, demonstrated publicly, and kept under check, i.e., both scandalous and safe.

Therefore, the marriage of a *tõ-sũguru* to another man is not considered unusual. It is celebrated by all the association in the traditional manner, and the *kamele*, who is bound at this occasion to pay for the cost of the party, is congratulated for having been the guardian of the girl, as in the village *flã-tõ*.

Indeed, many features of the *gũbe* are reminiscent of the traditional *flã-tõ*. It recruits among neighbors—the ward rather than the village—irrespective of traditional status and ethnic affiliation. Although it is not linked to the age-set system and to circumcision, it brings together children and youths of the same age-grade. As in the *flã-tõ*, the *gũbe* is under the supervision of a *tõ-ba* and a *tõ-fa* elected by the *tõ*. Even the *polisi*, as we noted for the *bara*, are not entirely the result of acculturation, since the existence of similar functions are noted in the *Komo* (Travele 1929). The rules relating to meetings and discipline derive from the traditional ones. The old village tradition of the youth entertaining the villagers is still present. *Gũbe* performances are public; people come to watch their children dancing and playing in a congenial environment. Even the relationships between the boys and girls are in part inherited from the *flã-bolo* custom of coupling the members of the two associations, without matrimonial prospects.

Nevertheless, these same social traits must be considered in the modern urban context, influenced by Western fashions. From this viewpoint, several of the *gũbe* customs become ambiguous. Western influence is perceptible even in the names that the associations take for themselves. Some names adopt exotic phonetics unknown in Bamana—such as *Jeunesse, Alliance, Esperance, Ambiance*—obviously in an attempt to sound foreign. Other names are chosen from sports teams (*Royal, Triomphe*) learned from the newspaper. These names express, of course, the desire of the young people to connect themselves with modernity and the prestige of foreign civilization. Clumsy imitation of administrative and bureaucratic fashions is found in the writing down, in French, of the rules which are given to the newcomers. The titles of the officials, as in many other types of association, are taken from the French bureaucratic hierarchy, except for the Almamy, which comes from Islam. Girls are expected to dress in the European manner; boys too wear European clothes—blue jeans and fancy shirts, with heel shoes and a "zazou" [33] haircut. Sometimes they wear a suit and tie. The president of the Niaréla *gũbe* always came dressed in a white suit.

Compared to the *bara*, relationships between boys and girls can be considered either as freer or as more conservative. In the *bara* boys and girls are matched into "monogamous" couples, once for all. In the *gũbe* a boy can have several *tõ-sũguru*, and the partners are changed or renewed every three or four months. Breaks in the relationship are more heavily sanctioned in the *bara* than in the *gũbe*. In both the girls have their choice. In spite of the fact that the *gũbe kamele* is entitled to a kind of "polygamy" (different from the custom in the old *flã-tõ*, but very like prevalent matrimonial customs), the rules can be

---

[33] Name given in the forties to the male adolescents in France, who distinguished themselves by their long hair, long coat, and narrow pants.

considered as introducing greater liberty into the relationships between the sexes, since they admit the possibility that it might not be permanent.

As in the *flã-tõ*, youngsters of all castes are taken in, but the lack of discrimination in the modern *gũbe* often results from ignorance or indifference. Partners are chosen without caste considerations, and in a few cases this leads to affairs or marriages between people traditionally forbidden to each other.

New values, linked to modern economic life, are replacing the old ones. A job and a money income have become the most important qualifications for membership. From that point of view and until lately, the *gũbe* was probably the most acculturated organization in the city, as it led toward a new social stratification of the associations of youth based on socio-economic considerations. The recruitment to each *gũbe* was determined more and more by the standing of the promoters, and youngsters of lower standing who were not admitted tried to create other organizations in the same ward or in neighboring ones. Of course, this tendency toward social stratification was hampered by the territorial bases of recruitment, and consequently did not work very well. The latest type—the club—has escaped this last restraint inherited from the traditional youth associations; the club furthermore rejects what was left of the traditional folklore.

The Clubs

Today's youth considers the *gũbe* to be outmoded and good enough only for the children. The modern young townsmen have organized themselves into clubs.

The first club was probably the Bourbon, which was created about 1953 by students home from France for their summer vacation and which centered around the ward of Médina-Coura.[34] The Bourbon introduced bee bop, a dance which was soon considered an essential element of "culture" among up-to-date young people. On the model of the Bourbon, another

---

[34] Médina-Coura was at this time considered to be of ill repute by the conservative people. There are still several "bars" and brothels in the ward.

club, the Triana, was founded around 1956 by modern young men who had *not* been to France—clerks from European firms, government employees, qualified workers, school teachers, musicians, children of rich traders, and others. Generally speaking, they were young men with money but of lower social standing, judging by modern criteria. Whether one had been a student in France was to become crucial for social standing. The monthly dues were set at five hundred francs. In addition, members were required to contribute two hundred francs for each party—called *intimité* [35]—and one thousand francs for the Christmas and New Year's Eve parties.

The example spread throughout Bamako, and numerous clubs were created hierarchically down the social scale and competitively at each level. It was not possible to compile a compete list of all the clubs, nor was the exact social definition of each available. During my stay in Bamako, I came to know of fourteen clubs.

One of these clubs originated in the *gūbe* described above. Seven boys from JBC II living in Dravéla got together informally and took the name of "Dean's Boys Club" (from James Dean). They showed great admiration for the American movie star, dressed in blue jeans and fancy shirts with plunging necklines, walked with hunched shoulders, and had their hair cut so as to look like their idol. Together with half a dozen girls from the former *gūbe,* they bought a tape recorder and organized modern dance parties.

The creation of Triana in the neighboring ward of Bamako-Coura in 1960 had aroused the interest of this group, and they had a talk about it, which soon turned into a debating session. Some members suggested that they gather all the youth of Dravéla into a similar club, but others objected that the boys and girls of the ward were *amorti* [36] and unable to dance prop-

---

[35] The French word *intimité* means intimacy. It is not used in metropolitan French to translate "party." The French slang among the youth is *surboum* or *partouse*. The colonial slang is *dégagement.*

[36] *Amorti:* a term in economics meaning depreciated, paid off, therefore used in French high school slang to mean "old." In Bamako the word is used by young Africans to mean "out of fashion," "numb."

erly, as could be seen at the Tahiti [37] anytime. After further discussion, they decided that in order to have as good a club as the Triana, they ought to enact some rules about membership. Two "laws" were therefore passed: (1) all candidates to membership must take a dancing examination, and (2) girls are forbidden to wear African clothes and flat sandals to the parties.[38]

Petitioners were requested to apply in writing. They were then invited to come to the club's *grẽ* in order to get acquainted with everyone. A girl proficient in dancing was unobtrusively appointed by the club to dance with them, so that the other members could judge the candidates without their knowledge. It was decided that to be elected, a boy had to know at least seven of the current dances (bolero, beguine, *rumba,* cha-cha, merengue, rock and roll, and the blues) or only two high-rated dances—the bee bop and the tango. Whoever knew the latter two dances was immediately accepted to full membership.[39]

Recruitment of girls was another problem. The objective was not to recruit just any kind of girl, but to get the prettiest ones in Dravéla. The only way to achieve this ambitious goal was to bring into the club S.K., the *kamele-kũ-tigi* of Dravéla. He was the "social leader" and a favorite among the girls of the ward. S.K. was a twenty-one-year-old blacksmith, one of those people who are said to be *dawla-tigi,* a man of appeal, not just to girls but to everyone. He and his friend also owned motorcycles, which had an irresistible attraction to girls. S.K. was therefore contacted. He agreed that he would gladly join, with the understanding, of course, that he would be elected *président.* Three days afterward, the organizational meeting was convened: nine young people from Dravéla and thirteen from Bolibana (the extension of Dravéla) were present. They

---

[37] A ballroom in Dravéla.

[38] There are no rules about the way boys dress, as they all dress in European fashion.

[39] It is assumed that Africans are usually good dancers. However, everyone in Bamako does not know how to dance, and those who are proficient have submitted themselves to intensive training, sometimes spending as much as two months in daily practice to learn one step perfectly. Good dancers are highly estimated as possible husbands by girls.

elected officers, with S.K. as *président*. The *vice-président* was a Guinean boy of twenty, the son of a kola merchant (a Kokoroko). The *secrétaire général*, twenty, from Bougouni, was an accountant (Manīka); the *trésorier*, born in Bamako, a mechanic of nineteen (Diawara); the *commissaire aux conflits* a college boy of twenty (Kagoro); the *organisateur*, a *kalādē* of a kola merchant, aged twenty-two (Suraka). One boy and one girl were appointed to the Committee on *Affaires Féminines* (recruitment and education of girl membership); the boy was nineteen, Bamako-born and an apprentice (Manīka); the girl, fifteen, was at school, and a Fulani. Only three of the officers had European educations, and a few did not speak French. They had, however, a regular money income either from their wages or from their work in family businesses. The two leaders were *ñamakala*. Entrance fees were set at five hundred francs for the boys—the girls did not pay this fee—and the monthly dues were two hundred francs for the boys and one hundred francs for the girls. They thus set themselves a lower standard than the Bourbon and hardly higher than the *gūbe*. The first money was used to purchase a record player and records.

S.K. was given the task of introducing the club to the adults of the ward in such an acceptable way that they would let their daughters join. The argument was that the purpose of the club was to bring together young people of two city wards arbitrarily divided by an administrative decision.[40] The first party was quite successful. After a speech by the *président*, the club was given the name of "Florina," from the name of a bar seen in a popular moving picture and close enough to the rival's name of "Triana."

The occasions for parties were many and were often linked to family events, as in the traditional associations, or to traditional and religious celebrations. Each dance was followed by a *réunion de critique*, during which every member, boy or girl,

---

[40] Dravéla grew toward the west into an extension called Dravéla-Bolibana, which became a separate administrative ward when it reached a population of several thousand people.

made comments and suggestions about the organization of the event, the attitude of the members, or related matters. During one of these meetings, a suggestion was made to organize a *thé dansant* to meet every Sunday afternoon from 3:00 to 7:00 P.M. An extra subscription of one hundred francs, or four bottles of soda pop, was asked every week for this purpose.

To begin with, no special rules regulated the relationships between boys and girls. When a boy joined with his girl friend, he only had to make it known that the girl was his. The unwritten rule was that boys and girls would form monogamous couples, friendly as well as amorous. Actually, a few boys tried to associate with several girls simultaneously, but they could not do it openly and had to hide their liaison to each of the other girls. It was said that more than two girls created "difficult diplomacy."

By 1962 the club had grown greatly and numbered thirty-four boys and about forty girls. It became so popular that everyone in the neighborhood wanted to join, and there was danger that the boys would outnumber the girls. Steps were taken to make the membership both selective and balanced. A third "law" was voted—no boy would be admitted without a girl, while single girls were of course always accepted. But rules relating to dress were even more strict. Girls were forbidden to wear wraparound skirts under their dresses or *pagnes* over their shoulders; short skirts and high heels were recommended; in addition, girls coming to the parties with the red dust of the street on their shoes would not be allowed in. Club money was used, therefore, to hire taxicabs during the evening parties, in order to pick up the girls in their pretty dresses and clean shoes. A boy was appointed to watch the entrance and turn away those girls who did not meet the standards.

The third law that no boy would be admitted without a girl created great concern and discontent among the youth of Dravéla, who wanted to be admitted precisely to be able to call on the girls of the club. One insider, B.K., tried to build up his popularity by taking the lead of the discontented ones from the outside. On the occasion of a baptism in his family, B.K.

invited the girls of the club, and he and his friends undertook to spread rumors about the attitudes of the girls' boy friends: either that one claimed that he did not like his girl but that she was hanging on to him; or that another one said that his girl slept with him every night; or that so and so's girl, who thought of marrying her club *kamele,* was nothing to him but a diversion, and so on. But the girls, after pretending to believe them and to quit the club, reported to the officers, who evicted B.K. and his friends.

At the same time that they made the club more select, the officers decided to create local sections in every ward. The girls, who had given proof of their loyalty, were considered the best asset for the success of the operation. In order to face the difficult problem of organization, a new official was elected to fulfill the function of *commissaire à la propagande.*

As it turned out, there was no time for the scheme to develop. In March, 1962, the club was dissolved after the following incident. For the *tabaski* celebration, each boy had contributed 750 francs for the purchase of food and drink. The money was entrusted to the *président* with instructions to buy one sheep, thirty chickens, bread, and soft drinks, and to pay various expenses, such as the fares of the taxicabs used for the girls. The total expense was less than the money collected, according to several members, but S.K. refused to give a detailed account, and, claiming that he had been offended, he resigned as *président.* During the dispute, he had been accused of acting as a dictator, but instead of taking steps accordingly most members said that they were tired of the club anyhow, and they dispersed without setting a date for the next meeting.

This event, however, did not herald the disappearance of clubs as a type of association. The members scattered, but they did not give up the spirit. The Dean Boys and a few girls went on dancing among themselves. Others joined various clubs in town, where they found themselves with Triana members, whose club, in the meantime, had also broken up. Later S.K. reconstituted the Florina with a new membership.

During the summer of 1963 clubs were numerous and active

in Bamako. I was invited to join three of them, in spite of the rules of exclusive membership. The three clubs were not situated on the same social level, though differences shade so imperceptibly that some people are of such standing as to be eligible in several of them.

The most select of the three was the Casa Antica. The majority of the members were educated—former college boys and girls with either the *brevet* (primary school diploma) or the *baccalauréat* (secondary school diploma). Only a few had been to France or to other countries, and then sometimes only for temporary visits and not for graduate studies. Those who had stayed for some length of time in France had been in provincial cities rather than in Paris. While I was in Bamako, several members, among whom was the *président*, were appointed as consulate clerks abroad. Many worked in the government; one was an airline steward and later a schoolteacher.

Below the Casa Antica came the Las Vegas, a majority of whose members were college boys and girls, therefore younger than the members of the previous club. Others were government clerks, several were surveyors from the Department of Statistics, or wage earners (mechanics, chauffeurs). Meetings took place at the shop of a young and successful tailor.

Ambiance [41] was more modest. Its members were an instructor in calisthenics, a barman, small government clerks, accountants, printers, and mechanics, but hardly any college people.

In spite of the social differentiation, common traits appear in all three clubs; some characteristics are similar to those we noted in relation to the Florina; others reveal changes in the direction of sophistication and social discrimination. Everyone is progressively turning toward European fashions: the latest dances are brought from abroad by students or travelers or are learned from repeated attendance at the movies. The rapid rate

---

[41] *Ambiance* was a fashionable word in the sixties. We know that it was also the name of the *jeli-tō*, of a Malian hit tune, and of fashionable native loincloth. Among Bamako youth, to be *ambiant* meant to be gay and lively. In the colloquial French of the teenagers in France, *ambiance* means "in the mood"; *ambiant* is not used.

of transmission is amazing—I have observed some short-lived fads in Bamako that I had not had time to learn in Paris. Dressing in the European way is *de rigueur,* although today African fashions seem to be more acceptable for girls, since they have become fashionable again in the highest circles.[42]

Consumption of liquor, mostly whiskey, has increased considerably—indeed, to the point of worrying the government about religious principles and the foreign trade balance. Restrictions have been put on the import of liquors, and prices have been raised.

The organization of the newer clubs seems to be less firm and tends toward de facto informal leadership. The Las Vegas, which is still the best organized, has six officers, but the tailor at whose shop they meet is the only active one. His function is to collect and spread the news and to serve as a clearing house. The entrance fee is theoretically set at three hundred francs plus four hundred francs for the cost of the record player. Monthly dues are two hundred francs. The contribution for the weekly *thé dansant* is one hundred francs for the full day or fifty francs for half a day. In addition, members share expenses in the event of a celebration.

In Casa Antica, there are only three officers. Periodical fees have disappeared and have been replaced by occasional collections, one thousand to fifteen hundred francs for celebrations. Such is also the case with *Ambiance:* leadership was given formally to the eldest, but he made no effort to exert authority, because no one would have taken such an attitude seriously. Erratic attempts were made to collect dues, but actually they were paid only when specific dance parties were planned.

All clubs, particularly the Las Vegas, claim that they still require a written application from prospective new members, who are submitted to a period of probation. I actually observed that in the other clubs, new members were introduced more often through informal introductions by one of the members.

[42] From 1960 on, the U.S.–R.D.A. has promoted a return to traditional clothing; this is not a move toward conservatism, but is in keeping with the evolving fashion in African dress.

The events celebrated as occasions for dancing changed in a very significant manner. In the Las Vegas—which is most keen to meet and dance on as many occasions as possible—they still celebrate marriages and baptisms of the members' kinsmen. But it has become more fashionable to celebrate the successes of members in school examinations or professional promotions and appointments. Several *intimités* were organized, often by the interested party and sometimes by girls, to celebrate a *brevet*, a scholarship to a foreign university, or an appointment to a consulate abroad. In addition, some clubs, whose leaders are known by high-ranking people, either Malian or foreign, are invited to private parties to bring in young people and spirits.

The ward is no longer the basis for recruitment. Members of a club are for the most part alumni from the same college or fellow workers. They actually live in various parts of the town. The Las Vegas, which has the youngest membership, is the easiest to locate; it covers three contiguous wards where the members formerly had met, played together, and attended the same local school. It is also partly an inheritance from a former ward *gûbe*. But the other two clubs have no territorial basis whatsoever, not even a permanent rallying point, except in the middle of town in the commercial section where everybody meets after work. Celebrations are given at members' places, wherever it is the most convenient each time, but with the idea that people must at some time invite the club to their own place.

Giving up familial celebrations in favor of those for individual promotions in a modern context, and abandoning ward affiliation in favor of modern social affinity mean that youth has achieved greater independence from elders, kinsmen, and the family in general, and therefore from the traditional modes of submissiveness.

The most radical and visible difference, however, between the club and other types of association is cultural. Not only have the clubs given up vernacular languages and adopted French for their names, titles, and bylaws, but in addition

English and other foreign words are showing up, following the metropolitan Anglomania. Literacy is required of the applicants; the notion of *examen*, borrowed from the French system of education, is brought in; a slang, derived from French but characteristic of the youth of Bamako, is in process of formation. Most of all, the folk dances, even in the changed and urbanized form of the *bara*, are openly rejected in favor of modern dances which are not altered, as in the *gübe*, but are adopted with concern about exact imitation. The boys are the instrument of this westernization; they impose it with great vehemence on the girls, especially in matters of fashion.

In this process the old values are left behind. Relations with families are loosened. Few clubs continue to celebrate the members' familial events. Parents are absent from the parties, and clubs do not put themselves under the control of elders. Instead, the members tend to celebrate each other's individual successes and to constitute a closed world; they are turned inward toward themselves, interested in problems which are their own and are not understood by their elders. One facet of this internalizing tendency is that entertainment has become strictly private. It takes place, not in the street as an entertainment offered to the neighbors, but inside the house for the exclusive benefit of the members.

This new world is being built on new principles, which are the essence of modern society. Having rejected the principles of family and seniority, the clubs are thoroughly penetrated by modern values. Money is the first criterion for recruitment. Entrance fees are so high that a primary selection is created between the rich and the poor. Beyond that, education and literacy are setting another scale: at the top are the members who actually stayed in Paris; the next echelon is made up of students from elsewhere in France or from another country; below them rank the educated young men from the local colleges. Ballroom dancing is a test in this up-to-date milieu: dances are introduced by young men who travel or, with some delay, those who see them on the screens of the expensive downtown cinemas.

The new hierarchy largely ignores relative age, and when, following the traditional mode, leadership is given to the eldest, it seems a weak and disorganized manner. The "social leader," the boy with poise and worldly wisdom, or the good "mixer" or good dancer may benefit from temporary leadership, but his leadership is not based on viable organizational principles. To the extent that officials still exist, any one who acts as a co-ordinator enjoys a pre-eminent position, but his leadership is sporadic, on the occasions of special events.

As the clubs become more selective, officers are less and less necessary. It is no longer relevant to state in the bylaws that candidates must be literate, and at a certain social level an examination becomes impertinent. Sophistication, and with it an etiquette of unwritten rules, is being substituted for a set of rigid laws.[43] Thus, at the highest social level, the clubs dissolve into increasingly narrow social circles and coteries, as the unwritten rules of recruitment become more and more selective. Indeed, the sophisticated way of life of the Westernized adult leaders, to the extent that it becomes known, stands as the norm of the new society and as the top of an uninterrupted social scale.

In the clubs relationships between the sexes are also affected by the new way of life, which is no longer regulated, but free. The notion of monogamous couples is implied. Open polygamous practices, as they still exist in the *gũbe,* are rejected, giving way to cunning "adultery." Boys are trying to fashion a new type of girl in accord with their vision of the world to which they aspire. The girls must be educated, well-dressed in the fashionable Western way, and good dancers. Clubs have created a new feminine social type: the *écolière,* as it is called currently, the schoolgirl, who in many instances, like the statue of Pygmalion, has escaped from her young makers.

Although this situation has led toward a quick emancipation of women and a deterioration of former matrimonial prohibitions, it has not yet set new rules in accordance with which this

[43] Invitations to parties are sent on special cards printed at expense by the Imprimerie Nationale.

liberation must take place. The *écolière* takes advantage of the role that she is asked to play. She dresses well, but also provocatively. She is the image of cultural achievement for the young men, but also for old men of position. She is desired both as a wife and as a mistress because she offers the double promise of modern social distinction and sexual license. Her apparent liberty presents a seductive challenge for the dominating male. Such potent attitudes toward greater emancipation are actively promoted by many girls, and in spite of many shortcomings provide a model for the young women of the rising bourgeoisie.

However, this attitude is more highly developed in Bamako than in other parts of the country. Liberty is understood in a more progressive way by girls and boys of the militant party organization of the youth. It would give a biased image of the modern youth to restrict our description to Bamako club activity. Let us add, furthermore, that the same people who attend the clubs sometimes also participate in the party youth organization. The present analysis is related to a social complex, to an institution, and not to individuals, some of whom belong to clubs and some of whom do not. The clubs represent a milieu leading to specific social phenomena, but the individuals are not rigidly linked to them.

Behind the apparent license and futility of the clubs, we can perceive a groping attempt to shape a new society, a new social order, and new sex relationships. At the moment the clubs stand as a refuge against the ancient society, as an exclusive rejection of its compulsions.[44] But the clubs also find themselves on the same ground as the new social leaders and therefore in competition with other groups which espouse the same modern values. The care to discriminate themselves from tradi-

[44] Positively, the clubs are opening the way toward breaking down the caste system through the absence of rules related to it. Liaisons can and do take place between young people belonging to groups traditionally forbidden to each other. However, within the club system this freedom might be easily deviated toward sheer sexual license and gives the *horŏ* boys an opportunity to have sexual intercourse without committing themselves. The more positive attitude is found only in the *Cercles culturels* of the Malian youth, in which such problems are debated and often given theatrical treatment as a means toward a constructive protest against social prejudice.

tion and the wish to compete, through imitation, with bourgeois society leads to fragmentation along lines that combine class discrimination and snobbishness. Money and education are the major criteria that create the growing split within the society at large; there is a tendency to confuse tradition with illiteracy and the African way of life with poverty. Beyond this major split, differences in degree, based on many criteria, parcel out the rising modern society into infinite fragments.

CHAPTER FIVE

Conclusion

THE various criteria, based on morphology and functions, adduced by sociologists to define a city are inadequate to characterize a place like Bamako. It is indeed a large concentration of people living in an uninterruptedly built area; it is a place fulfilling definite trading and administrative functions. But although these criteria locate Bamako within a process of urbanization, we must still come to appreciate the extent to which it is a city already.

Now, a city can also be defined by its inhabitants. A proper characterization of the townsman is, it would seem, as important as the definition of the city itself. For the sake of argument, one can define the "ideal" townsman from two points of view: as a man who has lost contact with the land, and as one who lives strictly by the market. The townsman has lost contact with the land on many counts: the land under his feet becomes smaller and smaller, and most of the time it lies several floors below him; the land is no longer the medium in which he works, for he does not cultivate it or get anything directly from it. The countryside (the land) is far away from the city man and is, for the most privileged, a place of rest and withdrawal. Economically, the townsman is entirely dependent on a money income, and he gets everything he needs through purchases on the market; he is entirely embedded in a money economy.

Applied to Bamako, this simple description hardly holds. The "land" is imported into the town: every compound is a reduced farmyard with cattle, poultry, and even fruit trees. Though only 10 per cent of the adult men claim to be agriculturists, many still cultivate the surrounding land or spend their week end tilling large fields borrowed from neighboring villages. An unknown but large portion of the food consumed in Bamako is produced by the inhabitants, and an even greater amount is brought in by kinsmen from the villages. Substantive economy is at the door. Relationships, we know, are frequent between city dwellers and their kinsmen in the hinterland. To go to the country is not to withdraw, or even to take a rest, but to return home and eventually participate in the agricultural work. Sole dependence on market economy has reached only a comparatively small portion of Bamako people.

Furthermore, the population of Bamako is new. As we have indicated, only a quarter of the inhabitants were born in town, and many of those stem from the original Bamako families who resist the trend of urbanization. Polygyny and illiteracy are higher in this group than others.

Bamako, therefore, can be seen as the meeting point of several rural currents: one stems from the inside, from the old Bamako village whose inhabitants remain villagers in reaction to changes brought in through foreign migrants; the others derive from the various hinterland areas and towns whose people strengthen their rural origins in order to assert themselves in opposition to each other.

These currents meet in the foreign frame of Westernized administration and business. Since the city is above all the point of impact of the Western world, the shift that we observe is not from a rural society to an urban one, but from an African way of life to a Western one. Bamako appears to be developing not from an inner force out of African society but from an abrupt and devastating contact with a foreign world. The "urban" way of life is imported.

Here, therefore, the very term "urban" refers to a phenomenon whose main constitutive elements not only are imported largely from the outside, but also remain unassimilated. These outside forces are still acting independently, with a tendency to exclude each other and little ability to merge into something qualitatively new.

Such an evolution, resulting from the contact of distant and radically diverse societies, takes a turn which is historically different from urbanization as it occurred in Europe. It is different from the modern metropolis which has become, for urban dwellers, a complete and comprehensive autonomous social milieu.

An image of these particulars is presented by the associations we have studied. Through some of them, the villages are carried in from the bush. Through others, the city is divided into village-like units. Others divide Bamako society according to various degrees of relationship with the European cities. The village associations value solidarity based on common origin and social distinction founded on birth. In the ward associations, belonging to the city is opposed to the rural origin, and personal status gives way to socio-economic achievement. Finally, in the clubs, differentiation comes from the urban society itself on the sole basis of Western values: money, education, and status seeking.

If a successful combination of the various constitutive elements should transform the city into something new and original, the *gũbe* could be considered as one of the most representative of "urban" manifestations. However, the fact that it is giving way to the clubs is a sign of failure to resist sheer Westernization.

The voluntary associations do reflect several important urban aspects. Through them the people approach such problems as social security, the need to create new social networks, to resist and break the ancient compulsions, and to solve problems of sex relationships in the modern context. Studying these associations helps pinpoint these problems and even gives a preview of what the city might become in the future. Yet the fact remains that associations cannot be fully explained without referring to the society at large. As we had to turn toward the hinterland to explain the city, so we have had to look away from the associations to find their roots and their purposes. We had to go back to the bush to understand and appreciate the folk dance associations, and we had to refer to Malian society at large and to the Western cities to illuminate the phenomena observed in the youth associations.

Voluntary associations, indeed, do not get to the bottom of the social problems. To observe their inner functioning for itself, without reference to the outside milieu, would have been to apply flatly the methods advocated by students of group dynamics but in a milieu which is not intuitively known, as is ours, by the investigator. If we had studied the associations from that restrictive and limited perspective, our interest would have centered on individuals inside the groups rather than on the groups in relation to each other within the larger society. We would not have studied them as a means of describing and understanding the society at large, but as an institution inside a society considered as *given,* which, precisely, it is not.

Voluntary associations, furthermore, are marginal institutions in relation to the society, and they are far from covering the entire—or even the fundamental—social needs of their members. The fact that their rules often try to bind the rank-and-file into their tight grasp is in itself a manifestation of their weakness. Yet in spite of the rules, people join and quit freely in response to personal problems that find their roots outside the associations. The social world that they try to reconstruct within these institutions is a factitious escape from the dominant social environment which, since it works and perpetuates itself, is the only one that is really binding. The associations do not actually succeed in perpetuating themselves. Many are short-lived and are linked to passing fashions. Belonging or not never comes to be as vital as belonging to the family or to an emerging socio-economic class. Now, none of the associations cuts along the fundamental social stratifications that we distinguished in the first part of this study; none follows the cleavage between the merchant and bureaucratic groups nor the division between the emerging social classes. The labor unions, the trade associations, and of course the various branches of the party are more significant from this point of view.

Voluntary associations, therefore, seem like bubbles rising and disappearing on the surface of boiling water. It is from deeper sources that the people who stir them find their motivation, and it is at more significant levels that we must try to explain a society in which associations are no more than indicators of social problems; reflections, to be interpreted, of some aspects of the society, but epiphenomenal too, because they furnish the points of convergence of many social forces. In Bamako, the "city" and the "urban" phenomenon still need to be approached from the outside. Urbanization is not yet a self-generating and irradiating process.

Glossary

ABBREVIATIONS:

Unless specified, the words are from the Bamana.
S = Sonïke; F = Fulfube; A = Arabic; Fr = French.

ba	large; river; mother
baba	ancestor
bãbado	caste of griots (F)
bala	xylophone; porcupine
bala-fo	playing the *bala*
balani	small *bala*
balani-dõ	dance to the *bala*
ba-moxo	people from the river; fishermen
bana	finished
bara	to work; a kind of round drum; dance ground; the cane carried by the *bara* dancers
bara-kamele	male companion in the *bara* association
bara-ñini	seasonal worker (*bara:* work; ñini: to seek)
bara-sũguru	female companion in the *bara* association
bele bele	very big
bila	kind of drawers made of a length of cloth wrapped around the waist and between the legs
bila-koro	wearer of *bila;* the uncircumcised
blõ	entrance to the ward, made of a cabin with one opening toward the outside and another toward the ward.
boli	to run
bugu	hamlet

ci	strength; life
ci-nama	a type of tilling association
cini	small, inferior
ci-wara	(*wara:* wild animal) mask worn during collective work of the association
cõpani	from the French "accompagnée"
cu	large drum used in the *segu-ka-bara*
da	mouth; opening; riverside; border
dabo	*griot* caste of the Jawãbe
dalamina	porte-parole
dawla-tigi	a man with appeal, charm
dẽ	child; dependant
dõ	dance
dõkela	dancer
dõso	hunter
drome	five francs
du	ward
dugu	village; country
du-kene	(*kene:* outside) yard inside the ward
dunũ-ba	large drum used in the *dunũba* dance
el hamdu-Allah	praise to God (A)
esusu	a Yoruba money-saving institution described by Bascom (1952)
fa	father
fara	skin
fara-je	white skin, white people, the Fula (*je:* white)
fasa	epic song
fere	the central square in the village, dancing ground
fila	two
fla	two
flã	people who belong to the same association of circumcized; twins
flã-bolo	group of circumcized of the same generation
flã-tõ	association of the circumcized of the village
flã-muso	girl from the *flã-tõ*
flã-muso-tigi	head of the girls from the *flã-tõ*
flã-tie	boy from the *flã-tõ*
flã-tie-tigi	head of the boys of the *flã-tõ*
fo	to greet; to play an instrument
foro	field
foro-ba	collective field
foro-ba-jõ	slave belonging to the community at large
fula-muso	Fula woman
fune	one caste of *griot*

gãgã	small drum
garãke	caste of cobbler (S)
gawlo	caste of *griot*
gelegelebani	drum used in the *segu-ka-bara*
gereñe	bell used by *griots*
gesere	*griot* (S)
gloki	garment for men
gloki-ba	large *gloki*
gõ	monkey
gõsõ	mask worn during the work of a tilling association
grẽ	informal meeting of friends
gũbe	association of the urban youth in the forties
gũbe-ba	mother of the *gũbe*
gũbe dẽ	member of the *gũbe*
gũbefo	performance of the *gũbe* to do honor to someone
gũbe kamele	male partner in the *gũbe* association
gwa	kins and affines eating regularly from the same pot
horõ	people of free condition and not casted
jãjõ	dance of the brave
jalã	dry
jamu	patronym
jare	*griots* of Manīka origin (S)
jãsa	a kind of dance for women
jazee	(from jazz) drum used in the *gũbe*
je	white, of light color
jẽbe	large drum played by popular musician
jeli	*griot*
jeli-dunu	cylindrical drum of the *griot*
jeli-dunūba	larger drum than the *jeli-dunu*
jī	spirit, genii; wall surrounding the ward
jīfutu	wall surrounding the house of the chief
jījebere	ginger beer
jõ	slave
jõ-ba	slave without master
jõ-ba-jõ	slave of *jõ-ba*
jula	merchant
jula-ba	important trader employing *jula-dẽ* and *jula-kaladẽ*
jula-dẽ	minor partner in trading business
jula-kaladẽ	apprentice merchant
juru-kele	(*juru:* string; *kele:* one) monocord guitar
kalã	to learn; to read
kaladẽ	learner
kamele	young man of the age to be married
kele	one; single

ko	to speak; to wash; small river
komo	a secret society; slave (S)
kono	bird; inside
kora	harp-like instrument of the *griot*
kore	a secret society
koro	beside; old
Koteba	farcical theater
kũ	head
kura	new
kurusi	large baggy pants
kũtigi	chief
la	place (suffix)
laobe	caste of the woodworker (F)
latikeli	drum used in the *gũbe*
latikeli-kela	drummer of the *latikeli*
mabube	caste of weavers (F)
marka	Bamana name of the Sonĩke
medersa	school (A)
Medina	town (A)
mine	to take
mise	small
misi	buffalo
moĩni	millet porridge
monrovia	gauze overdress
mori	marabout
muniã	house of the chief
muso	woman
nama	a secret society
ñamakala	casted person
ñaxamala	casted people (S)
ni	diminutive (suffix)
ñini	to look for
n'tomi	tamarind
n'tomo	ruined settlement
numu	caste of smiths
pagne	loin cloth (F)
pari	money saving institution (F)
pĩpõ	drum used in the *gũbe*
rimaibe	slave (F)
rĩbe	free person (F)
saba	three
sabar	a kind of dance and association (Wolof)
sãsani-tõ	tilling association
segu-ka-bara	former dance of the Masasi; an association of youth

	in Bamako
semi, sẽbi	harp-like instrument of the hunters
senene	to till
senene-tõ	tilling association
sere	witness
sigi	to be seated
sigi-sigila ka	people who hesitate
so	horse; house
sofa	rider; horseman
sogo	meat; game
sogonĩ-kũ	head of the *sogo*
soku	violin
suk	market (A)
sũguru	girl of the age to be married
suraka	moor
tabaski	moslem celebration (Easter)
tage, take	caste of smiths (S)
taille-basse	feminine dress (Fr.)
tama	drum of *griot*
tana	prohibition
tata	fortification
tegere	bandit; to clap hand
terike	friend
tẽtẽ	drum used in the *gũbe*
tibrĩgeñe	third-generation slave
tie	man
tõ	rule; association
wailbe	caste of smiths (F)
wara	wild animal
wene	whip
wolo	to be born
wolo-so	domestic slave (born in the house)
yayoba	acrobatic dance

References

Amin, S.
1963   *Schéma d'étude sur l'économie du Mali.* Institut de Dé-
            veloppement Economique et de Planification, Dakar.
            Annuaires du Gouvernement Général de l'AOF (1900,
            1922).
Annuaires Statistiques de l'AOF
1923, 1960
Anonymous
n.d.   "Monographie du Cercle de Bamako." Typed, Archives,
            Koulouba.
Ba, A. H., and J. Daget
1962   *L'Empire peul du Macina.* Vol. I, Paris, Mouton.
Balandier, G.
1955   *Brazzavilles Noires.* Paris, A. Colin.
Banton, M.
1957   *African City: A Study of Tribal Life in Freetown.* Ox-
            ford, Oxford University Press.
Bascom, W.
1952   "The Esusu. A Credit Institution of the Yoruba," *J.R.A.I.,*
            82.
Bouche, D.
1949, 1950 "Les villages de Liberté en AOF," *Bulletin de l'Institut
            Français d'Afrique Noire,* 11, No. 4:491–540; 12, No.
            7:135–215.
Bouffard, Dr. G.
1908   "La défense de Bamako contre la fièvre jaune." *Bulletin
            de la Société de Pathologie Exotique* I:7.

156   References

Brasseur, G., and G. Savonnet
1960, 1963   *Cartes ethno-démographiques de l'Afrique Occidentale.* (Feuilles No. 2, 3, 4.) Dakar, Institut Français d'Afrique Noire.

Caillé, R.
1830   *Journal d'un voyage à Tombouctou et à Djenné, dans l'Afrique Centrale pendant les années 1824, 1825, 1826, 1827 et 1828.* Paris, Imprimerie Royale.

Centre d'Etude Sociologique
1953   *Villes et Campagnes* (ed. G. Friedmann). Paris, A. Colin.

Chailley, M.
1962   "Aspects de l'Islam au Mali (1958–59)," in *Notes et Etudes sur l'Islam en Afrique Noire.* Recherches et Documents, Centre des Hautes Etudes d'Afrique Musulmane:9–52.

Cissé Y.
1964   "Notes sur les sociétés de chasseurs malinké," *Journal de la Société des Africanistes,* 34, No. 2:175–226.

Clément, P.
1956   "Introduction à l'étude des Associations Volontaires," in *Aspects Sociaux de l'Industrialisation et de l'Urbanisation en Afrique au Sud du Sahara* (ed. D. Forde).

Collomb, Dr.
n.d.   *Notice sur le Cercle de Bamako.* Unpublished MS in the Archives, Koulouba, Institut des Sciences Humaines.

De Ganay, S.
1956   "Le *to,* société d'entr'aide chez les Bambara du Soudan Français," in *Actes du Ve Congrès International des Sciences Anthropologiques et Ethnologiques.* Philadelphia.

Delafosse, M.
1909   Monographie du Cercle de Bamako. MS in the Archives, Koulouba (not complete).

1910   "Monographie historique du Cercle de Bamako," *Renseignements Coloniaux,* No. 3 (supplément to *L'Afrique Française* [Mai], 57, 67).

1912   *Haut-Sénégal-Niger, le pays, les peuples, les langues, l'histoire, les civilisations.* Paris, E. Larose.

Denis, J.
1958   *Le Phénomène Urbain en Afrique Occidentale.* Bruxelles, Académie des Sciences Coloniales, Bruxelles, Mémoire, T. XIX, fasc. 1.

Dieterlen, G.   "Mythe et organisation sociale au Soudan Français,"

1955   *Journal de la Societe des Africanistes*, XXV, No. 1–2:
                39–76.
Dresh, J.
1950   "Villes d'Afrique Occidentale," *Cahiers d'Outre-Mer*
                (July–September), 11:200–230.
Ecole Pratique des Hautes Études
1963   *Les Villes* (entretien interdisciplinaire sur les sociétés
                musulmanes). Paris.
El Bekri
1965   *Description de l'Afrique Septentrionale.* (11th century.)
                Paris, Maisoneuvre.
Forde, D. (ed.)
1956   *Aspects Sociaux de l'Industrialisation et de l'Urbanisation
                en Afrique au sud du Sahara.* UNESCO.
Gallíeni, Col.
1885   *Voyage au Soudan Français* (1879–81). Paris, Hachette.
George, P.
1962   "Matériaux et réflexions pour une politique urbaine
                traditionnelle dans les pays en voie de développement,"
                Tiers-Monde (July–September), 11:337, 60.
Gosselin, M.
n.d.   *Bamako.* Typed. Paris, Centre des Hautes Etudes
                d'Afrique Musulmane.
1953   "Bamako, ville soudanaise moderne," *Afrique et Asie*,
                No. 21, 31–37 (summary of above).
Government Publications
1958   *1907–1957: 50e Anniversaire de l'Assemblée Consulaire.*
                Bamako, Chambre de Commerce.
1960   *Etude démographique de la République du Mali: Rap-
                port provisoire.* Ville de Bamako. Duplicate. Bamako,
                Min. du Plan, Dir. de la Statistique.
1961a   *Etude d'Aménagement de la rive droite du Niger.* Typed.
                Bamako, Ministère des Travaux Publics, SEMA–SCET.
1961b   *Rapports politiques (1884, 1921).* MS in the Archives,
                Toulouba.
1962a   *Comptes économiques de la République du Mali.* Paris,
                Min. de la Coopération.
1962b   *Enquête sur les cultures maraîchères à Bamako.* MS
                Bamako, Min. du Plan, Dir. de la Statistique.
Graves, H.
1907   "Bamako, capitale du Haut-Sénégal et Niger," *Questions
                Diplomatiques et Coloniales* (January–June), 23:571–76.
Herbe, P.
n.d.   "Rapport sur un plan d'urbanisme de Bamako." Typed.

158   References

Holas, B.
1953   "La Goumbe," *Kongo-Overzee*, 19, No. 2, 3:116–31.
Hopkins, N.
1964   "The Modern Theater in Mali." *Committee for the Comparative Study of the New Nations Seminar*. Chicago.
Irani, H.
1962   *Contribution à l'étude des transports au Mali*. Duplicate. Bamako, Min. des Travaux Publics.
Kamian, B.
1959   "Une ville de la République du Soudan:San," *Cahiers d'Outre-Mer* (July–September), 47:225–50.
1963   "Les villes dans les nouveaux Etats d'Afrique Occidentale," *Tiers-Monde* (January–June), 13, 14:65–80.
n.d.   *Connaissance de la République du Mali*. Bamako, Secretariat d'Etat à l'Information.
Labouret, H.
1934   "Les Mandingues et leur langue," *Bulletin du Comité d'Etudes Historiques et Scientifiques d'Afrique Occidentale Française*, 1:270.
Lasserre, G.
1958   *Libreville et sa région*. Paris, A. Colin.
Leynaud, E.
1961   "Les Cadres sociaux de la vie rurale dans la Haute-Vallée du Niger." Typed. Paris, Bureau d'Etude pour le Développement de la Production Agricole.
Little, K.
1957   "Role of Voluntary Associations in West African Urbanization," *American Anthropologist*, 59:579–96.
1960   "La Ville dans l'Ouest Africain," *Diogene* (January–March), 29:20–37.
1962   "Some Traditionally Based Forms of Mutual Aid in West African Urbanization," *Ethnology*, 1, No. 2:197–211.
Mauny, R.
1959   "Evocation de l'Empire du Mali," *Notes Africaines* (April), 82:33–37.
1961   *Tableau Géographique de l'Ouest Africain au Moyen Age*. Dakar, Institut Français d'Afrique Noire.
Meillassoux, C.
1963   "Histoire et institutions du kafo de Bamako, d'après la tradition des Niaré," *Cahiers d'Etudes Africaines*, 14:186–227.
1964   "The *Koteba* of Bamako," *Présence Africaine*, 52:28–63.

1965   "The Social Structure of Modern Bamako," *Africa* (April), 35:125–42.

Meniaud, J.
1912   *Haut-Sénégal-Niger:Géographie économique.* Paris, E. Larose.
1931   *Les Pionniers du Soudan.* Paris, Société des Publications Modernes.

Ministère de la Marine et des Colonies (France)
1884   *La France dans l'Afrique Occidentale, 1879, 1883.* Paris, Chellamel.

Monteil, C.
1915   *Les Khassonke, monographie d'une peuplade du Soudan Français.* Paris, E. Leroux.
1924   *Les Bambara de Segou et du Kaarta.* Paris, E. Larose.
1929   "Les Empires du Mali, étude d'histoire et de sociologie soudanaise," *Bulletin du Comité d'Etudes Historiques et Scientifiques d'Afrique Occidentale Française,* 291–447.
1953   "La Légende du Ouagadou et l'origine des Soninke." Dakar, IFAN, Mém. No. 23:359–408.

Mougin, J.
1947–48   *Bamako, hier, aujourd'hui, demain.* Typed. Ecole de la France d'Outre-Mer.

Ortoli, J.
1936   "Les Bozo," *Bulletin de Recherches Soudanaises* (October), 4:152–78.
1939   "Coutume Bambara (Cercle de Bamako)," in *Coutumier juridique de l'A.O.F.,* t. II (Soudan), 127–60. Paris, Larose.

Paques, V.
1953   "L'Estrade royale des Niaré," *Bulletin de l'Institut Français d'Afrique Noire* (October), 15:4.

Park, M.
1954   *The Travels of Mungo Park.* London, Everyman.

Prouteaux, M.
1929   "Premiers essais de théâtre chez les indigènes de Haute-Côte d'Ivoire," *Bulletin du Comité d'Etudes Historiques et Scientifiques d'Afrique Occidentale Française,* 12:448–75.

Saint-Père, J. H.
1925   *Les Sarakollé du Guidimaka.* Paris, E. Larose.

Sembene, O.
1960   *Les Bouts de Bois de Dieu.* Paris.
1962   *Voltaïque.* Présence Africaine.

Sidibe, M.
1958   "Bamako, ville de rencontre," *Festival Afrique* (July 21), 1.

Sjoberg, G.
1960   *The Preindustrial City*. Glencoe, Ill., The Free Press.

Tauxier, L.
1927   *La Religion Bambara*. Paris, P. Geuthner.
1930   "Chronologie des rois Bambara," *Outre-Mer* (June), 2, No. 2:119–30; 2, No. 3:255–66.
1937   *Moeurs et Histoire des Peuls*. Paris, Payot.
1942   *Histoire des Bambara*. Paris, P. Geuthner.

Traore, D.
1947   "Sur l'origine de la ville de Bamako," *Notes Africaines* (July), 35:26.
1948   "Une seconde légende relative à l'origine de Bamako," *Notes Africaines* (October), 40:7.
1950   "Les origines de Bamako," *Le Soudan Français* (December 29), 17.

Travélé, M.
1928   "Note sur les coutumes des Chasseurs Bambara et Malinké du Cercle de Bamako," *Revue d'Ethnologie et des Traditions Populaires*, 9:207–12.
1929   "Le Komo ou Koma," *Outre-Mer* (June), 1, No. 2:127–50.

Tricard
n.d.   *Etude sur la coordination des transports au Soudan*. Duplicate. Bamako, Min. des Travaux Publics.

Urvoy, Y.
1942   "Petit Atlas ethno-démographique du Soudan entre Sénégal et Niger." Dakar, Institut Français d'Afrique Noire, Mém. 5.

Vallière, Chef de Bataillon
1888a   Carte de la Mission Gallieni, 1/1.000.000 (Kayes-Ségou-Bamako). Archives Nationales d'Outre-Mer, Paris.
1888b   *Mémoire sur le Cercle de Bamako*. MS. in the Archives Nationales d'Outre-Mer, Paris.

Weber, M.
1958   *The City*. London, Heinemann.

Zahan, D.
1960   *Sociétés d'initiation Bambara*. Paris, Mouton.

Index

Amadou (chief of Toucouleur clan), 6, 7

Ambiance (club), 136, 137

Ambiance (dance association), 107–12

Amin, S.: cited, 3, 9*n*, 12, 22, 24*n*

Annuaires Statistiques de l'AOF: cited, 9*n*

Apprentices and mates, 36, 74; mentioned, 34

Association d'Entr'aide de Dar-Salam (mutual aid association), 84

Association des Artistes du Mali, l'Ambiance. See Ambiance (dance)

Associations: aboriginal, 49–50, 54; boy-girl relations in, 51, 106, 115, 127–34 *passim*, 140–41; colonial, 58–61; defined, 49–50, 146–47; fees, 62, 63, 79, 81, 85, 104–8 *passim*, 114, 121–22, 131, 133, 137; functions, 51–52, 54, 60–61, 62–63, 74–79 *passim*, 85, 98, 105–6, 119, 127, 133; meetings, 52, 77–78, 89, 123–25; organization and officials, 51, 70–72, 77–78, 81–82, 85, 92–93, 97, 100, 104, 107–8, 113–25 *passim*, 132–33, 135, 137, 140; post-colonial, 69–70, 73, 141–42, 145–47; recruitment criteria, 51, 58–62 *passim*, 76–77, 83–97 *passim*, 120–23, 132–42 *passim*;

registration required, 57; role in urbanization, 54, 75–76, 93, 105–6, 116, 129, 130, 139–42, 145–46; statistics, 58-67 *passim*, 131; mentioned, 95, 97. *See also* specific kinds of associations: Clubs; Dance associations; Esoteric societies; *Gūbe;* Labor unions; Mutual aid associations; Official associations; Old men's associations; Regional associations; Religious associations; Social promotion associations; Sports associations; Youth associations

Ba, A. H.: cited, 48

Bagadadji (city), 84–86, 118

Bamako (city): center of government, 7, 8, 13; city planning, 9, 10, 15; compared with ideal, 144; economic roles, 4, 8, 13, 19–24 *passim*, 144; geographic position, 4, 20; growth rate, 9, 13; history, 3–15; military roles, 7; number of inhabitants, 3, 9–17 *passim*, 41; population density, 12, 15; sections, 6, 8–9, 14; vital statistics, 18; mentioned 24

Banque de la Republique du Mali: cited, 24

Women: associations for, 84–86;
dancers, 103, 110; entertainments
for, 89; new image, 140–41; sources
of income, 84

Workers, seasonal (*bara-ñini*), 39–40;

associations for, 92, 93, 97

Youth associations, 50–52, 64–65, 71–
72, 120–21

Zahan, D.: cited, 52